Style City
LONDON

StyleCity
LONDON

With over 400 color photographs and 7 maps

Thames & Hudson

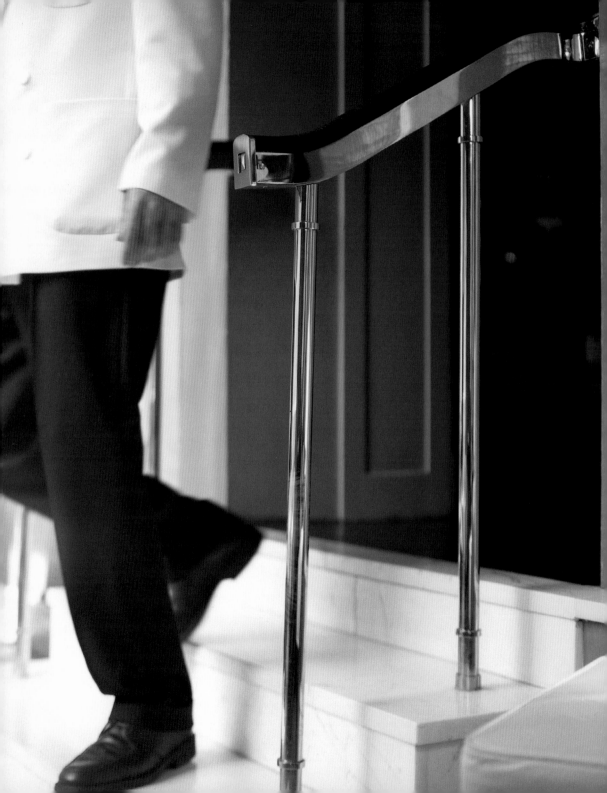

Contents

Series concept and editor: Lucas Dietrich
Research and texts: Phyllis Richardson
Jacket and book design: Grade Design Consultants
Original design concept: The Senate
Maps: Peter Bull

Specially commissioned photography by Ingrid
Rasmussen, Anthony Webb and Francesca Yorke

Except p. 145 courtesy Tom Aikens restaurant

The StyleCity series is a completely independent guide.

Every effort has been made to ensure that the
information in this book is as up-to-date and as
accurate as possible at the time of going to press,
but some details are liable to change.

This edition published in 2005 in paperback in the
United States of America by Thames & Hudson Inc.,
500 Fifth Avenue, New York, New York 10110

thamesandhudsonusa.com

Library of Congress Catalog Card Number 2004110565

ISBN-13: 978-0-500-21013-0
ISBN-10: 0-500-21013-6

Printed in China by C & C Offset Printing Co Ltd

The book features two principal sections: **Street Wise** and **Style Traveller**.

Street Wise, which is arranged by neighbourhood, features areas that can be covered in a day (and night) on foot and includes a variety of locations – cafés, shops, restaurants, museums, performance spaces, bars – that capture local flavour or are lesser-known destinations.

The establishments in the **Style Traveller** section represent the city's best and most characteristic locations – 'worth a detour' – and feature hotels (**sleep**), restaurants (**eat**), cafés and bars (**drink**), boutiques and shops (**shop**) and getaways (**retreat**).

Each location is shown as a circled number on the relevant neighbourhood map, which is intended to provide a rough idea of location and proximity to major sights and landmarks rather than precise position. Locations in each neighbourhood are presented sequentially by map number. Each entry in the **Style Traveller** has two numbers: the top one refers to the page number of the neighbourhood map on which it appears; the second number is its location.

For example, the visitor might begin by selecting a hotel from the **Style Traveller** section. Upon arrival, **Street Wise** might lead him to the best joint for coffee before guiding him to a house-museum nearby. After lunch he might go to find a special jewelry store listed in the **shop** section. For a memorable dining experience, he might consult his neighbourhood section to find the nearest restaurant crossreferenced to **eat** in **Style Traveller**.

Street addresses are given in each entry, and complete information – including email and web addresses – is listed in the alphabetical **contact** section. Travel and contact details for the destinations in **retreat** are given at the end of **contact**.

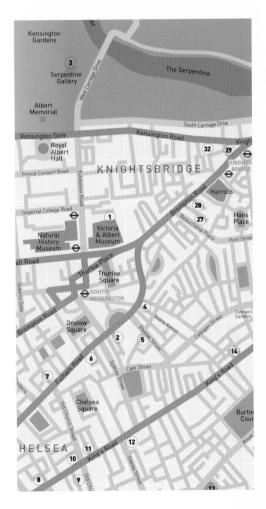

Legend

2 Location

Museums, sights

Gardens, squares

Metro stops

Streets

LONDON

Like many cosmopolises, London is heterogeneous and multilayered, complex and contradictory. According to a 2000 United Nations census, London's greater metropolitan area included around seven and a half million inhabitants, making it the 26th largest city in the world. Although it may not be one of the globe's top ten most populous cities, it is arguably the most diverse and among the most culturally influential. Bridging the United States and Europe in many, often conflicting, ways, and being the capital city on an island, as opposed to a continent, have imparted to London a number of curious qualities that have often insulated it from (if not made it resist) the larger continental forces across the Atlantic and the English Channel.

Intensified by a dense historic urban fabric that has been fractured by the Great Fire of 1666 and the Second World War, London's political, cultural and social spheres have a potent way of intersecting and mixing. Unlike many larger European cities, which have grown concentrically out from a historic (usually medieval) centre of power, and most American cities (except Los Angeles), which are based on the democratic grid, London is a concatenation of essentially autonomous villages that have merged over time. What were once royal hunting grounds in the 17th century or new suburbs in the 19th have been subsumed into the greater whole that is London today.

The result is that London has not one heart but many. With the exception of the Mall, London is unmarked by the grand urban gestures of Pope Sixtus V's Rome, Haussmann's Paris or Cerda's Barcelona, which created axes rather than centres. London's composition of mainly smaller streets and lanes feels distinctly unmodern, unimposing and accessible – a pedestrian paradise. Whereas most visitors regard the main tourist sights – Trafalgar Square, Buckingham Palace, St Paul's Cathedral – as central London, for Londoners there is no true centre, except perhaps the high street of their neighbourhood. There are financial centres (the City) and cultural magnets (the West End), but in the main London is everywhere. The best way to experience everyday London is in its villages.

The millennium has seen an efflorescence of *grands projets* in the capital, which has revivified the worlds of the arts, design and fashion and substantiated the 'Cool Britannia' image beyond the media. Perhaps the most successful and popular of these recent catalysts is

Tate Modern (p. 101), which has awakened the British populace's largely guarded attitude towards contemporary art, provided visitors to the city with a genuinely modern cultural destination and stimulated a neglected part of London, the South Bank. Moreover, there are less-publicized but equally important cultural institutions that are enjoying new leases of life: the intimate National Portrait Gallery has been significantly expanded with a new wing (which includes a restaurant providing unparalleled views over the city; see p. 148). The Royal Opera House (p. 54) has been refurbished, enlarged, modernized and incorporated into a lively tourist destination, the Covent Garden Piazza. The British Museum has been restored to its original 19th-century form and the Great Court reinstated under architect Norman Foster's canopy of glass. Somerset House (p. 57) has been reinvented and restored and its several major art collections brought back to life. A number of smaller museums, often overlooked by visitors to the city, have also been renewed and extended since 2000: the Wallace Collection in Marylebone (p. 63), for example, enjoys an atrium designed by Rick Mather.

But perhaps no buildings symbolize the city's optimism and 21st-century outlook more than the Greater London Authority (G.L.A.) building, also by Foster, and the London Eye, designed by Julia Barfield and David Marks, on London's South Bank. With their curvilinear forms on prominent riverside positions and their manifest high technology and transparency, these buildings signal London's openness to modernity and new forms of expression.

Yet, while the face of London may be enjoying a public restoration, the most dynamic element of the city remains its thriving, though less visible underground scene. New trends in music, fashion and art that gain global popularity are often the product of London's subcultures rather than its established institutions. At the turn of the millennium, London images of 'street style' have as much influence on the world as they did in the 1960s. Inspired by an edgy, vital youth culture and the broad spectrum of ethnic influences, London's creative scene continues to confirm the city's position as a world leader.

As with any great city, it is impossible to distil London's essence; even life-long inhabitants are unable to characterize the city's complexity, to reconcile what is English versus what is international. But London thrives on the very contradictions it creates, the borders that it blurs. Visitors wishing to experience London beyond its tourist destinations will discover its idiosyncrasies, its uniqueness and its timeless appeal in the places that follow.

Street Wise

Notting Hill • Holland Park • Kensington • Knightsbridge •
Chelsea • Mayfair • Soho • Covent Garden • Marylebone • Fitzrovia •
Bloomsbury • Holborn • Clerkenwell • Islington • King's Cross • City •
Brick Lane • Shoreditch • South Bank • Southwark • Bermondsey

Notting Hill
Holland Park
Kensington

Walking around the designer-label shops and trendy cafés of Notting Hill today, you would never suspect that as late as the 1950s this was one of London's most impoverished areas, nor would you immediately recognize that it is the centre for the city's Afro-Caribbean culture. The latter distinction is celebrated every August Bank Holiday weekend, when the Notting Hill Carnival swings into gear and around two million people pour into W11 and W2 for days and nights of colourful pageantry, dance music and street-fair fun. When its gentrification began some years ago, Notting Hill became known as the home of 'Trustafarians' (trust fund + Rastafarian), those twenty- and thirty-somethings who emerged from their privileged backgrounds and/or private schools in search of a kind of bohemia, albeit luxurious. So, although gradually regenerated over the past decades and brought into the world's public consciousness by a movie starring Julia Roberts and Hugh Grant, Notting Hill represents a determined effort to preserve the air of an arty-funky lifestyle.

Fortunately for year-round visitors, the atmosphere epitomized by the Notting Hill Carnival can be experienced more than once a year. Every weekend the antiques market on Portobello Road, the area's spiritual and geographic backbone, adds a suitable dash of gritty urbanism and multicultural vibe while providing useful hunks of old Victoriana, with enough wear and tear to make it obvious they didn't come from the grandparents' manor house. Shops and pubs lining the north end of Portobello Road represent the new blood in Notting Hill in terms of talent and artistic edge. All Saints Road, once known for its laid-back, drug-induced groove, is today an almost idyllic enclave, with street-smart eating, drinking and shopping all along a couple of blocks. Some of the area's more adventurous places are around the junction of Westbourne Grove and Needham Road; whereas the convergence of Westbourne Grove and Ledbury Road is a smorgasbord of new-era designers, galleries and eateries that could easily hold you in thrall for an afternoon.

Farther south, the largely residential and seriously upscale areas of Holland Park and Kensington need little introduction. The quarter's centrepiece is Holland Park itself, providing one of those grand oases of green space in which London rejoices. Whereas so many localities of London are famous — or infamous — for their energy and verve, Kensington is the pure embodiment of English gentility, urban-style, but, like so many of the capital's neighbourhoods, just another village with a style all its own.

1 Olivia Morris
355 Portobello Road

She's hit the fashion press with her vibrant concoctions in materials like plum leather with glitter 'peeled' toes, pink moiré tango sandals and red suede high-belted knee boots. Olivia Morris studied shoe design at the well-known Cordwainers College cobbling school. Soon after she was working for the likes of DKNY, Boyd, Evisu and Patrick Cox, all the while creating her own line of footwear. Her shop at the top end of Portobello Road gives only a hint of what's inside with samples sitting seductively in a window obscured with black curtain. It's not until you get inside that you get the real idea of Olivia Morris: quirky, witty and unabashedly sexy. Flourishes, such as removable bows, satin, glitter or mirror details and her trademark silver lining have made her shoes distinctive and recognizable. Morris has also created an accessible collection for Topshop while at the same time collaborating with hot fashion duo Preen (see below) on their latest catwalk show, as well as with designer Matthew Williamson (see p. 47).

ANTIQUES AND BRIC-À-BRAC

2 Portobello Road

One of London's most popular street markets, Portobello Road has evolved from its late-19th-century association with gypsies' trading horses, and is today known for its stalls of antique furnishings, prints and accessories that attract tourists and collectors from around the world. The shopping starts to get interesting north of Chepstow Villas. Some of the stalls are offshoots of existing shops, but a good many are independent, with quality varying from real finds to those with more than a fair share of whimsy. The market is also full of clothing, music and a jumble of other items. It's perhaps the carnival atmosphere that is most appealing and only happens on Saturday (though shops are open six days a week). A very pleasant way to pass the morning and perhaps uncover a treasure or two.

CIVILIZED CLUB CULTURE

3 Number 10
10 Golborne Road

With its smart, Déco-inspired bar serving breakfast, lunch and an extended list of gins and sherries, a member's bar and a white-clad formal restaurant on the first floor, Number 10 reaches out beyond expectations to offer clubbers a more civilized atmosphere for their revels.

While the house and guest DJs churn out respectable techno-ambient tunes, with special events on Sundays, the other floors are given over to more social and gastronomic pursuits. The self-proclaimed 'not a bar; not a gastropub' wears its '1950s ski chalet-Dada magazine-Regency wallpaper' décor well. Settle in and enjoy dinner from the inventive menu, while perhaps listening to some live classical music, or rise up and dance.

VINTAGE STREET

4 Rellik

174

HORIZONTAL LOUNGIN'

5 Bed Bar
310 Portobello Road

A spacious young bar at the top end of the Portobello market's gamut of stalls, the Bed Bar is as relaxing as it sounds. Traditional wobbly wood chairs have been thrown out in favour of large banquettes covered in brightly upholstered cushions. Downstairs, lounging is encouraged, while upstairs, proper tables and a separate cocktail bar invite more involved conversations. The atmosphere is casual and the service upbeat. A good place to while away an afternoon with a pint or sprawl out of an evening.

STUDIO PLAY

6 Under the Westway

156

YOUNG AND INSPIRED

7 Portobello Green
281 Portobello Road
• Preen, no. 5
• Baby Ceylon, no. 16
• Zarvis, no. 4

Under the cover of the Westway flyover an arcade of small boutiques with the unlikely appellation of Portobello Green is tucked away off the busy Portobello Road. There is not much green here, but there are plenty of other colours to attract you among the array of young designers. The fanned and pleated new Victorian-style designs of Preen, for example, have engaged a celebrity following; Baby Ceylon has womenswear in softer floral patterns and pastels. Be prepared to be drawn in to Zarvis, whose cornucopia of scented oils, salts and body treatments fragrantly overflows with temptation.

ROAD TO FASHION

8 Portland Road

- Julie's, no. 135
- Virginia, no. 98
- The Cross, no. 141

Portland Road becomes a villagey collection at Notting Hill's north end, which provides a taste of stylish neighbourhood life. Virginia attracts vintage addicts from all over London with its collection of lacey Victorian and latter-day delicates. Its straw hats and flowers are mirrored by the romantic conservatory seating at Julie's across the way, a restaurant that has long been a favourite with the locals and features themed rooms soaked in candlelight by night. Up the road a little farther you'll find another destination for London designers and celebrities. As well as carrying new British designer clothing by independent labels like Goat, The Cross sells those little accessories that speak volumes in fashion language.

FLOWER POWER

9 Cath Kidston

8 Clarendon Cross

British designer Cath Kidston's Notting Hill shop is a bower of bright prints and flowers in a distinctly crisp English style that has been much praised for its witty and nostalgic appeal. Vivid floral patterns, as well as bold polka dots and stripes, are splashed across everything, from aprons to ironing-board covers, pillows to tablecloths. Her fabrics are also available.

THE ART OF VINTAGE

10 Mary Moore

5 Clarendon Cross

Daughter of sculptor Henry Moore and trendsetter in her own right, Mary Moore has recently opened a shop selling top-quality vintage clothing in this little fashion hub on the border of Holland Park and Notting Hill.

Nadia Demetriou Ladas's Notting Hill tableware shop and gallery is the result of an obsession. Ladas began collecting 1950s glassware after visiting the glass-blowing region of southern Sweden. Today her commitment to contemporary design is evident in the Scandinavian pieces, Italian art glass and works by important British designers such as Tom Dixon and Nigel Coates and sculptor Anish Kapoor. 'Everything in the shop has been chosen with passion', she explains, and 'all fit into Walter Gropius's definition of good design, that they should have beauty, quality, function and affordability'. The shop was designed by Ladas's partner, furniture designer Angel Monzon.

Already a London institution for movie mavens, the Electric has made itself even more popular with a refurbishment by Nick Jones, the man behind members-club Soho House and the artful Babington House near Bath (see p. 180). An amazing glass frontage conceals a feat of restoration and refinement that has resulted in marvellously comfortable leather armchairs with footstools and tables to hold your movie snacks in the theatre. There is also an updated bar, open half an hour before screenings and serving wine, beer, champagne and cocktails, as well as 'substantial cinema snacks'. It all adds up to one of the most comfortable and satisfying nights you will ever have at the pictures. If you can't eat at the bar, the Electric Brasserie next door offers formal and casual dining from burgers to fresh seafood: a good place for a post-film chat with friends.

14 Trailer Happiness

HERE COMES THE NEIGHBOURHOOD

15 All Saints Road
- Ashbells, no. 29
- Uli, no. 16
- Manor, no. 6–
- The Jacksons, no. 5

Mixing Notting Hill off-beat funky with more upscale tendencies, All Saints Road, a two-block enclave and a short distance from the touristy Portobello Market, is a microcosm of the best of west London. Near the top end of the street is the recent arrival Ashbells, with soul food inspired by the American south. If Carolina-style pulled pork with creamy grits, southern-style chicken livers with fried onions or Maryland crab cakes are on your mind then you'd better stop here, as nowhere else in London is likely to answer your craving, or at least not as well. The hip nightspot Manor has maintained a regular following in an area where bars come and go with the fashion collections. The booths are comfy, the drinks are well mixed and the crowd is always lively. Much-loved English retro-hip designers The Jacksons have a white-painted corner shop full of highly coveted shoes, bags, scarves and belts. Their street-wise fashions are featured in other London design shops but here you can see the whole range. Thai-Chinese restaurant Uli is an acclaimed neighbourhood gem with the added surprise of a garden in the back.

REAL MUSIC

16 Rough Trade
130 Talbot Road

From the outside it looks like many an independent record shop still catering to devotees of vinyl but Rough Trade is a genuine British institution among music lovers. It began as a shop devoted to Jamaican and American music in 1976 and soon became associated with the punk movement in the UK. Expanding to include record producing, distribution and publishing wings, the Rough Trade label weathered a number of musical highs and lows, including a successful association with the Smiths and the later collapse of the distribution and publishing companies. But through it all the shop remained a focal point for hearing and acquiring new music. Remaining true to their 'punk ethos', Rough Trade were among the first UK outlets to promote bands like the White Stripes, and they take real

pride in the pursuit and discovery of innovative sounds. For vinyl and CDs, modern classics, hard-to-get and brand new hot-off-the-press releases, or just to see what's happening in new music, wander in for a listen.

NEIGHBOURHOOD JOINT

17 The Cow

THE OUTDOOR LIFE

18 The Westbourne
101 Westbourne Park Villas

The Westbourne is one of those places that looks so inviting and appealing that trying to resist a swift half is futile. Perhaps it's the outdoor terrace, usually filled with youthful locals, or the quiet, tree-lined setting somewhat removed from the area's buzzier streets. A reincarnation of an old neighbourhood boozer, with large forecourt and wood-filled interiors, it boasts a modern menu and attractive clientele that are happy to be in the know.

THE SPICE ROAD

19 Blenheim Crescent
- The Spice Shop, no. 1
- Books for Cooks, no. 4
- Blenheim Books, no. 11

This small street holds a wealth of literary and other surprises. Birgit Erath started with a weekend spice stall on the Portobello Road. At the Spice Shop she now stocks over 2,500 products and is a source for many a top London chef, who come for her hard-to-find spices and her expert advice. She also dispenses the latter at events held at Books for Cooks, across the road. It's not only a centre for gastro-publishing but the café in the back serves well-prepared international dishes all culled from the tomes on the shelves. However, it's lunchtime only and they don't take bookings. Blenheim Books is a popular source for books on everything related to the green arts, from planting to landscape design.

ginger

DUC
A
MP

The Royal Borough of Kensington
LEDBURY
ROAD, W.11.

20 Ginger

115 Westbourne Grove

A bright new-style Asian restaurant, Ginger will make you stop and stare over its silvery booths and turquoise chairs. Another reason to stop is that its kitchen genius, Albert Gomes, was head chef at one of Bangladesh's most luxurious hotels and his aim is to bring speciality Bangladeshi food, not just the umbrella Indian style, to London. Fried red pumpkin, duck and mango curry and Bengali fishcakes are just some of the unusual and wonderfully prepared dishes that cover the range of fish, seafood, chicken, lamb and a particularly lauded biryani.

LEATHER LUXE
21 Bill Amberg

175

SCENT-SATIONAL
22 Miller Harris

14 Needham Road

Lyn Harris is the young perfumer behind this very highly regarded line. After working with perfume-makers in Paris and Grasse, she launched her own range with the help of perfume house Robertet, who helps manufacture her very distinctive collection. Basing many of her perfumes on 'old-fashioned, naturally derived' aromas, which are more expensive to work with than synthetics, she creates complex concoctions such as 'Coeur Fleur', a mix of sweet pea, mimosa, Egyptian jasmine, raspberry, peach, Florentine iris, amber and Madagascan vanilla. The beautifully designed shop also houses her scent garden, 'full of roses, jasmine and herbs', which customers are encouraged to visit. Harris offers a bespoke service consultancy, inviting clients to access her fragrance library and laboratory to create their own personal fragrances. Look sharp, though, as this service is currently booked more than six months in advance. A new shop recently opened on Bruton Street in Mayfair.

REDEFINING DECORATIVE ARTS
23 Flow

1–5 Needham Road

Opened in 1999 to 'showcase the best of British contemporary applied arts', Flow was established by Yvonna Demczynska, who had worked as a dealer in British crafts in the US and Japan. With an interior that is clever but not overwhelming, the work of the gallery's

40 represented artists, working in ceramics, glass, wood, textiles, basketry, metal and jewelry, is displayed on floating white shelves. Look out for Kate Allsop's architectural works in porcelain, Amy Cushing's glass tiles using materials developed in the space programme and nature-inspired metalwork by Kim Harrell.

MAGICAL JEWELRY
24 Solange Azagury-Partridge

171

NEIGHBOURHOOD CHARM
25 Ledbury Road

- Duchamp, no. 75
- Fiona Knapp, 178A Westbourne Grove
- Simon Finch, no. 61A

Ledbury Road is a fulcrum of the Notting Hill scene, charming with a parade of small, idiosyncratic shops. Mitchell Jacobs at Duchamp specializes in men's dress-shirts, ties, cufflinks and socks with decided flair. Jacobs has a real penchant for strong colour, so you will find candy-coloured shirts in three different cuff designs (casino, double and two-button) paired with ties full of texture and bright, contrasting hues in modern patterns, as well as geometric, jewel-set cufflinks.

New Zealand-born Fiona Knapp's blackened jewel box on the corner of Ledbury Road shows off her innovative metal arts in settings like sprays of fireworks or bold, coloured stones set together. Her 'Mosaic' collection was inspired by Byzantine and Baroque churches, while the seductive shop interior dressed in black velvet and amethyst silk, took its cue from the film *The Leopard*. Next door Anya Hindmarch (see p. 37) has her second shop selling her signature bags, and also shoes and other accessories.

Simon Finch has been trading in antique and second-hand books since his university days. This shop, opened in 1999, demonstrates the success of his commitment with a techno-modern design by Marina Chan of AMP that displays his collection of 20th-century literature and photography titles. His earlier shop on Maddox Street in Mayfair still brims with the wide range of his stock.

REGALIA FOR FEET
26 Emma Hope's Shoes

162

SUBTLE DISTINCTION
27 Dinny Hall

170

DREAMY DRAPERY
28 Ghost
36 Ledbury Road

Tanya Sarne's drapey, dreamy creations have been accumulating applause and fashion awards since 1990. Designed, as she says, 'by women for women', they are intended to make every woman feel beautiful. Sarne eschews hard lines, concentrating instead on 'how a fabric feels against the skin'. To that end, her vintage crepe, velvet and satin, for example, are put through a special production process to achieve their sensuous flowing quality. The shop in Ledbury Road is her flagship store, which reflects her unique blend of relaxed femininity.

HOME FROM HOME
29 The Main House
 128

COCKTAILS AND . . .
30 The Lonsdale
 155

SOUTH AMERICAN FUSION
31 Wall
1 Denbigh Road

Peruvian Hernan Balcazar and his British-born wife, Judith, have brought the riches of Andean fabrics to London with inventive flair. As creative director, Judith Balcazar works with in-house designers to create women's clothing that is comfortable as daywear and elegant enough for evening. From T-shirts to linen jackets and alpaca coats, the pieces signify 'simplicity, luxury and comfort'. Using blends of handpicked cotton, alpaca and vicuña, the pieces tend towards neutrals in summer and warm contrasts in winter, such as dark cinnamon and cherry.

PLEASING DELAY
32 Windsor Castle
 154

PLEASANTLY CROWDED
33 The Havelock Tavern
57 Masbro Road

This popular pub restaurant is somewhat off the beaten track, but it shows how consistently good food and a lively atmosphere can maintain a success story. The staff are relaxed, the interior doesn't try too hard and everything from the steak and chips to the fried monkfish is fresh. Be warned though: fresh food runs out, and they do not accept credit cards.

A PRE-RAPHAELITE GESAMTKUNSTWERK
34 Leighton House Museum
12 Holland Park Road

The former studio-house of the high Victorian artist Frederic Lord Leighton (1830–96) is a spectacular paean to 19th-century decoration and craftsmanship, with an exotic Eastern flavour that was popular among Leighton's artistic circle. Leighton took up residence in 1868 and continued with the embellishment until his death. Among the house's many treasures are perhaps the finest collection of tiles by William de Morgan and a theatrical Arab Hall complete with fountain, elaborate mosaic floor, cupola and stained glass. Leighton's meticulous drawings and some of his paintings, as well as others by contemporaries Edward Burne-Jones, John Everett Millais and George Frederick Watts are in the collection.

AGEING GRACEFULLY
35 The Scarsdale Tavern
23A Edwardes Square

In one of Kensington's most exclusive neighbourhoods, less than a minute from Kensington High Street and filled with bright-white Georgian terraced houses, is an enchanting public house with a façade that looks straight from a chocolate box. No commercial reproduction this – it's an age-old favourite of the well-heeled locals who savour the good food and quiet, homey atmosphere.

TIMELESS CLASSIC
36 Maggie Jones
6 Old Court Place, Kensington Church Street

In the face of the epicurean revolution that has taken hold in London, Maggie Jones's menu, which has changed little over 40 years, is something of an institution. Thankfully, this has less to do with tradition and more to do with how reliably good the food is. Prawn cocktail, avocado and smoked chicken for starters, and fish pie and poached salmon are among the regulars on the menu, with specials that change daily. With the charm of fresh flowers, colourful funky crockery and well-worn wood furniture, it's hard not to feel comfortable here.

INDIAN CUISINE REIMAGINED
37 Zaika
 142

Knightsbridge
Chelsea

With the vast, lush green expanse of Hyde Park to the north and the gleaming Chelsea Embankment to the south, the largely residential areas of Chelsea and Knightsbridge are probably the most picturesque and stereotypically preserved areas of London. Chelsea's immaculate terraced houses dripping with purple wisteria in the summer and Knightsbridge's high-end shopping create a patch of what can only be described as incredibly civilized London.

The spirit and symbol of Knightsbridge for most visitors is Harrod's, which still holds a certain cachet as a purveyor of luxury and designer-brand goods. For locals, however, it is the smaller, more intensively stylish department store Harvey Nichols, at the top of Sloane Street, which emerged during the 1990s as the vanguard of the younger set whose parents shopped at Harrod's. Rather than providing the feeling of a grand old country-house larder, Harvey Nichols's upstairs food hall is contemporary and sleek.

Harrod's and Harvey Nichols might reflect the tension between tradition and modernity that gives so many parts of London their edginess, but Knightsbridge's creative side is driven by the presence of the Victoria and Albert Museum (p. 30), whose magnificent collections have ensured that the surrounding area has what must be one of the highest concentrations of fabric and upholstery stores and interior designers in the world. Although the character of much of the area's design remains at the traditional end, there are clear signs that attitudes are changing: a new architecture gallery at the V & A and adventurous programming, catalyzed by a team of young curators, offer ever more exciting exhibitions. Increasing globalization has brought modernity to classic sensibilities in the interior decoration realm as well – Kit Kemp's Knightsbridge Hotel (p. 122) and David Collins's Blue Bar (p. 150) are great examples.

Ever since the King's Road made a splash in the 1970s, Chelsea's shops and designers have continued to present their particularly English take on high style and fashion. The shops along Sloane Street are dominated by predictable global fashion labels, so those seeking funkier boutiques and more adventurous outlets should head to King's and Fulham Roads. But seek out the smaller streets, like antiques-shop-lined Walton Street, Beauchamp Place (p. 38) or Pont Street (p. 37), because they capture Chelsea's charming character and the quintessence of classical – or modern-traditional – English design more than anywhere else in the capital.

GARDENS OF DELIGHT

1 Victoria and Albert Museum

Cromwell Road

PRINT HAPPY

2 Ginka

137 Fulham Road

The largest museum of applied and decorative arts in the world needs little introduction. You might see only one collection – 'Clothing through History' in the Dress Gallery, for example, or the splendours of the Asian and Islamic Art collection. You might spend a lot of time staring at the Great Bed of Ware in the grand, not-to-be-missed British Galleries (1500–1900) – with pieces by Chippendale, Morris, Mackintosh, Wedgwood and Liberty – or Lord Leighton's frescoes after having visited his astonishing house (p. 25), or the magical Glass Gallery. Whatever you manage to see, no visit should be without a stroll through the Pirelli Garden, an Italian-style piazza garden set within the late-19th-century walled courtyard. A large central fountain gurgles beneath swaying trees: in summer a tented enclosure serves refreshments and visitors can enjoy the garden and museum until 10 pm on Wednesdays.

Textile designer Neisha Crosland has split her business between home furnishings and fashion with the former located around the corner on Elystan Street and this little shop dedicated to her vibrant and highly original range of clothing and accessories. It's given her room to expand, and she now produces two fashion collections a year. Her skirts, tops, jackets, jumpers and scarves all feature the sharp graphic motifs that she has become known for in expertly contrasted colours and textures. Handbags, too, in various sizes, complement the vivid schemes of her clothing designs, and notecards and wrapping paper demonstrate just how sharp an eye for pattern she possesses. If you desire unique Crosland prints on a larger scale, wallcoverings and furniture fabrics are on display at the Elystan Street premises.

3 Hyde Park
Serpentine Gallery

The largest of the royal parks, Hyde Park's vast green space in the centre of the city contains pockets that each have their particular beauty: from the classic English Rose Garden and romantic 19th-century statuary and an Italianate folly to the Princess Diana Memorial park, one of London's most imaginative play areas, and Speaker's Corner, a magnet for public soapbox-style debate since 1855. Occupying a former tea house is the Serpentine Gallery, which presents world-class contemporary art exhibitions in a more relaxed setting than the severity of so many of the city's galleries and museums. Most summers an internationally renowned contemporary architect is invited to create a folly for the lawns in front of the museum; recent years have seen works by Zaha Hadid, Daniel Libeskind and Toyo Ito (shown above).

AL FRESCO OYSTERS AND CHAMPAGNE

4 Bibendum Oyster Bar
Michelin House, 81 Fulham Road

Designer and entrepreneur Terence Conran has been an influential part of the British restaurant scene ever since he opened his Soup Kitchens in the 1950s. Design and food have combined in a number of widely publicized restaurant ventures by the design guru, but one of his earlier – and most lasting – eateries is located in the Art Nouveau Michelin Tyre headquarters (architecturally interesting in its own right). While upstairs is the formal Bibendum restaurant, the ground floor features an informal seafood bar and restaurant serving a wide variety of oysters, caviar and *fruits de la mer*, in a patio-like setting next to a bright flower stall.

REFINED DINING

5 Tom Aikens

145

Simon Wilson has been designing costume jewelry for over 25 years, and some of his better-known pieces are creatures – the 'lazy lizard', 'slinky serpent' and 'friendly spider'. But there are also the delicate drop earrings and pendants in soft pastels, gems that are displayed alongside the shop's array of vintage items, which includes a selection of antique Scottish jewelry, Art Déco pieces in silver, semiprecious stones and marcasite and a treasure trove of one-off bags – beaded, box-shaped and zippered. The retro-looking turquoise-wash exterior makes the shop leap out from the parade of upmarket boutiques on the Fulham Road, promising something inviting and altogether more fun.

Robert Emmett started out as a tailor but then became 'dissatisfied with the imperfections of off-the-peg shirts' and began making his own shirts 'with discerning taste and tailoring them to the highest standard'. He sources fabrics all over the world and has the shirts made to his designs in Italy. The 400 designs available each season boast details such as contrasting panels under collars and cuffs, and only 25 shirts are produced to each design. Choose from double (French) cuffs, single cuffs and casual shirts in unusual patterns and textures; a hint of something tailor-made but not trying too hard to get noticed. He also makes men's pyjamas and boxers. A line of women's shirts is soon to be launched.

British glass designer William Yeoward set up this sparkling shop on Chelsea's King's Road in 1996 with the ingenious idea of creating reproduction English Georgian (18th century) crystal for purchase off the shelf or by special order. Stem- and barware, jugs, decanters, plates and vases are all handblown and handcut to historic patterns, many in fine floral designs. Yeoward also presents a refreshingly modern take on reproduction tableware, with a bright-looking purple shop and prices that range from an unintimidating £25 for a hand-crafted wine glass. Yeoward has also launched a homewares collection at no. 270.

Emily Dyson says that her signature is in the detail, rather than in the grand design, and that is what catches the eye at Couverture, a shop dedicated to well-designed bedclothes and bed-linens. Formerly a designer for British fashion leader Paul Smith, Dyson identified a gap in the market for the kind of finely trimmed linens you might associate with antique or vintage articles, and then presented them with a thoroughly modern attitude. While the shop is awash with white and pale shades, closer inspection reveals a velvet cuff on a silk pyjama bottom or dressing gown, or a needlework-patterned hem on sheets and pillowcases that impart that satisfying hint of luxury. Couverture also carries select items by other designers.

Designer Tricia Guild's King's Road mecca for vivid and contemporary home furnishings and fabrics stocks an array of objects from furnishings to greeting cards; but what makes her place so appealing, apart from the Mediterranean colours that mark her collections, is that every piece is the work of a named designer or craftsperson. Since 1970 she has been amassing the work of artisans, from abroad and locally, to create an exceptionally vibrant selection, a breath of fresh air in a design scene dominated by grey modernistas. Long a favourite of designers and design publications on the hunt for something original, Guild has a proven (and well-published) track record for finding appealing objects and talent. As you look through the assortment of beautifully printed wallpapers, colourful woven and embroidered linens, hand-made ceramics, glassware and accessories, you may very well find yourself swearing off mass-produced and flat-packed furnishings for good.

A delicate and unusual green space, the Chelsea Physic Garden has been a home to specimen and medicinal plants since 1673, when it was planted as the Apothecarie's Garden for educating apprentices in the identification of plants. The riverside setting was chosen for its milder climate, which would support non-native species, and the first greenhouse in England was built here in 1681. Though away from tourist attractions, the Physic Garden is well worth a detour, especially when it is combined with a walk along the Chelsea Embankment or a look at the nearby Chelsea Royal Hospital, designed by Sir Christopher Wren in 1692.

'A paradise of *passementerie*' is how Annabel Lewis describes her breathtaking assortment of fine ribbons, bows, tassels and beads. Now V.V. Rouleaux is a single-stop destination for trimmings for clothes, furnishings – just about anything that could do with a flourish or a touch of colour or sparkle. The eye-catching crepe, organdy and silk ribbons, flowers, braids and countless other irresistible ornaments are all as appealing as wrapped candy.

Jo Malone celebrated ten years as the top name in British personalized skin care in 2004. Her minimalist black-and-white labels are now recognized and prized in and beyond Britain, but her products are still designed for the needs of the individual. Malone encourages 'fragrance combining', so all of her 15 original fragrances can be layered with others to create an entirely personal scent that can be tested in the shop's fragrance booths.

C3a RED CHECK PJS

C7b STRIPED PJS

C7a LAWN PJS

Designer Tracey Boyd has lit up the catwalks with her bright, slim-fitting clothes that range from feminine prints to textured linen to jeans and corduroy. Boyd's own-label shop presents a cool, fashion-conscious face to Elizabeth Street, home to several high-ranking boutiques and cafés. This is the definitive source for Boyd's increasingly popular vintage-inspired line, which has attracted Liv Tyler and Kate Winslet, among others.

Her handbags have animated the pages of *Vogue*, *Cosmopolitan* and *Elle*, they've adorned the arms of Madonna, Björk and Elizabeth Hurley. But Lulu Guinness is no slave to fashion: she makes fashion all her own. Call them whimsical, naive or cartoonish, but her floral prints, 'house' design or signature 'flowerpot' bags are instantly recognizable. Colourful, bright and delightful, her shop has irresistible sweetshop appeal. If her designs remind you of 1950s Parisian fashion plates, that's just one example of old-style glamour that inspires Guinness.

The Peruvian-born, London-trained designer has a seeming love affair with texture and colour. A creator of luxurious scarves and feminine accessories, Georgina von Etzdorf made her name in the early 1980s with seductive combinations of rich velvets, supple silks and delicate chiffons in sumptuous blends of colour. Her womenswear combines hand-embroidery, silkscreening and finely crafted detailing on a range of tempting fabrics. Though her designs are distributed through a number of worldwide outlets, her London shop is the place to really experience the enveloping von Etzdorf effect.

A short row of boutiques just off the well-traversed Sloane Street, Pont Street is a cluster of indigenous creative design talent. Elspeth Gibson's appointment-only shop is filled with her desirable wispy romantic pieces. Hemlines can be highish, and many of the fabrics diaphanously sheer. Made famous by her custom swimwear, Liza Bruce's taste is for the loose, unstructured garment. The shop also carries modern furniture designed by her husband, Nicholas Alis Vega. Rachel Riley has taken traditional-style children's clothes and sweetly refined them with hand tailoring and beautiful fabrics worked in her atelier in France. The results are a nod to the 1950s in crisp cottons and linens, bright polka dots, stripes and custom prints. Riley makes clothes for women as well.

Anya Hindmarch found her style niche at the age of 19, when she discovered the fondness Italian women had for simple drawstring bags. Her designs are colourful, witty and well-crafted: photo-print beach scenes look like vintage postcards and beaded mosaic pop-art bags, such as the 'Heinz Baked Beans' bag with a beaded 'label' stitched on to a tin-shaped denim carrier, have become classics. In 2002 she launched a shoe collection, for which she produced green pumps and a matching bag featuring a striking reproduction of a Rose's Lime Juice label.

The sultry screen idol Gina Lollobrigida was the inspiration for this sexy line of footwear that began in the 1950s. Gina shoes are still made in East London, and the designs are still slinky, feminine, as popular as ever with the fashion-minded and continue to express a certain kind of female glamour.

Along this street of genuine luxury, lingerie legend Janet Reger, who has produced supremely seductive intimate apparel since the 1960s, beckons from no. 2. Sitting somewhat incongruously amid high fashions is the Map House, a source of fine antique maps, globes and engravings for almost a century. Try a drink at Townhouse, a chic-funky bar and restaurant where you can recline in leather sofas to sip a lemongrass and chilli martini.

Opticians Graham Cutler and Tony Gross transformed eyewear from necessity to fashion statement over 30 years ago, inspired, they say, by 'the British love of non-conformity'. Their world-renowned designs are available at their original London premises, designed in 1969 by Piers Gough, where they still do eye exams. A second shop sells vintage C&G designs and classics by YSL, Courreges, Christian Dior, Brigitte Bardot and Pucci.

Designers Maureen Doherty and Asha Sarabhai create clothing that can be worn by young and old in relaxed styles that are luxuriously well-made in India using traditional weaving and stitching techniques, from designs based on traditional work garments to those inspired by 17th-century Indian menswear. They also have exhibitions of largely British contemporary craftspeople.

Mayfair
Soho
Covent Garden

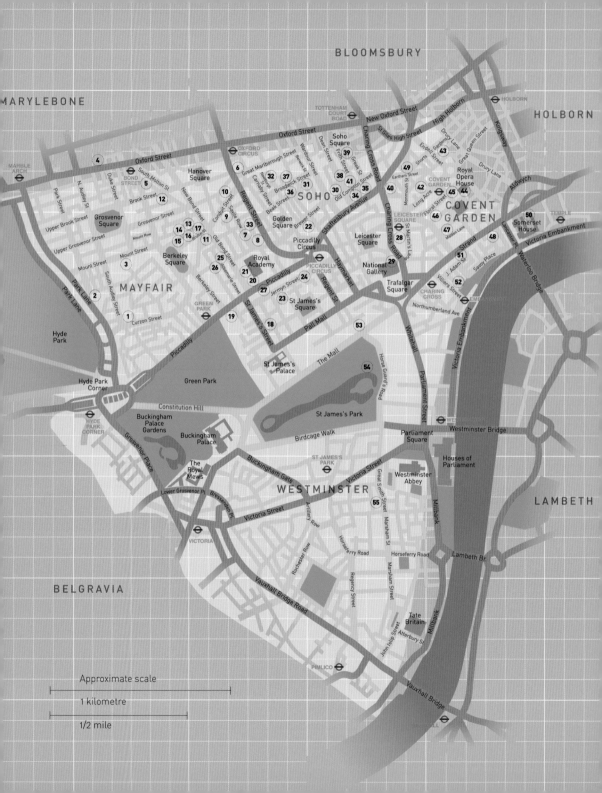

Inevitably and somewhat inexplicably, most visitors to London make their way to Leicester Square, Piccadilly, Regent Street, Covent Garden Piazza. In their own way, each of these places represent for many people London's energy, its metropolitan air, its buzz. Stripped of their local colour, over-illuminated by neon, overpopulated by unthinking tourists and often infiltrated by gaudiness, many parts are now little more than symbols of former greatness, their grandeur denuded by the globalizing monoculture. Get quickly away from these magnets and you are in the heart of the West End – dense, chic, lively and ever-changing.

West of John Nash's wonderfully grand Regency boulevard, Regent Street, is Mayfair's dense concentration of high style and fashion, art and commerce. Bisected by Bond Street – lined with a mixture of international fashion labels and classic old shops and galleries – Mayfair is true-blue upmarket London, a genuine oasis of gentility between Piccadilly and Oxford Street. Many of the shops, auction houses and galleries – and therefore also the restaurants and bars – cater to a small group of the wealthy and well-heeled, but there are pockets of affordability for all of us. If you've allowed for a one-off extravagance, this is the place to indulge.

Crossing Regent Street going east, you are unmistakably in Soho, flashy and seedy, creative and degenerate, hip and outmoded. The first sign is the once-cool-now-downmarket Carnaby Street, a resonant reminder of how changes in fashion are accelerated in the city centre (though running parallel one street away, Newburgh Street [p. 51] is alive and well). Although the area's high density of media and creatives maintain Soho's buzz during the day, and recent pedestrianization has made it a generally pleasant place to stroll, its primacy as London's liveliest night spot is slipping eastwards, toward Hoxton Square and Shoreditch. Soho is still buzzing, and according to Kevin Spacey, new director of the Old Vic theatre (see p. 105) 'changes character more frequently than a schizophrenic method actor in a one-man show'.

Since its gentrification in the 1970s, when its old vegetable market was moved to south London, Covent Garden has attracted a largely youthful crowd with its numerous bars and many designer boutiques selling the latest streetwear. With the refurbishment and expansion of the Royal Opera House, however, an older, more culturally inclined group demanding higher standards of food and drink has had an impact. The Palladian-style Piazza, designed by Inigo Jones in 1635, is the quarter's centrepiece and tourist mecca, but the small streets and alleyways that surround it have much to offer – if you know where to look.

GENTLEMANLY GROOMING
1 Geo F. Trumper
9 Curzon Street

While men's grooming habits and styles have wavered over the past century, Trumper's commitment to professional service, for which they have been awarded six royal warrants, has not. Still occupying beautiful period premises, the shop that began catering to London gentlemen in 1875 offers a range of services, from haircuts to facial cleanses to chiropody. They even conduct a 'shaving school' where you can learn the best technique to use at home. Trumper's own range of toiletries are on gleaming display in front, while the full menu of treatments, including the ever-popular wet shave with open razor, are performed at the back of the shop by the waistcoat-wearing professionals.

ARCHETYPAL CARVERY
2 The Grill Room at The Dorchester
136

PEACEFUL RESPITE
3 St George's Gardens
Off Mount Street

This wonderfully secret, enclosed green space laid out as a public park in the late 19th century is surrounded by grand Queen Anne–style houses and shaded by giant plane trees. Small, discreet wrought-iron-gated entrances near Carlos Place mean the gardens are usually a peaceful, unpopulated place to sit on a wooden bench and take in the scenery. In the south-east corner is the Church of the Immaculate Conception, known as the Farm Street Church, built in 1849 for English Jesuits and containing a high altar by Pugin, architect of the Houses of Parliament.

ONE-STOP ULTRASHOP
4 Selfridges
166

BRITISH FASHION IN FOCUS
5 Browns + Brown Focus
23–27 and 38–39 South Molton Street

There are many places to buy designer wear in London, but few have the cachet that Browns has achieved over the past three decades. Joan Burstein and husband, Sidney, opened the shop in 1970, and since then it has become a revered name in London fashion. Browns features well-known designers from all over the world, while Browns Focus, across the street, demonstrates Burstein's prescient eye for young innovators, which is evidenced in the shop's 2001 design by one of Britain's most in-demand architects, David Adjaye. Fake London, Frost French, Hussein Chalayan and Maharishi are just a few of the talents showcased.

THE ART OF CRAFT
6 Liberty
214–20 Regent Street

Arthur Liberty opened his shop on Regent Street in 1875, and his mock-Tudor building soon became one of the most fashionable shops in London, drawing such artistically inclined clients as Pre-Raphaelites Edward Burne Jones and Dante Gabriel Rossetti. The store has a long association with crafts (they still have a partnership with Moorcroft), employing Arts and Crafts and Art Nouveau designers to create pieces that are still famously 'Liberty' in style. The ground floor of the Tudor Shop (built in 1924) houses the sumptuous haven of the 'Scarf Hall', where you can find Liberty designs, such as the ostrich-feather pattern, as well as pieces by well-known designers and up-and-coming talents. The lower ground floor is home to Liberty's signature array of crafts pieces and the rather groovy Arthur's café.

REINVENTING SARTORIAL ELEGANCE
7 Savile Row
165

BESPOKE MASTERY
8 Ozwald Boateng
166

DESIGN BY ORDER
9 Oki-Ni
169

THE EPITOME OF STYLE
10 Sketch
140

11 Asprey
167 New Bond Street

'British luxury goods since 1781' says the store motto, and the Asprey label is still going strong. The flagship store opened in May 2004 under the guidance of new creative head and top designer Hussein Chalayan, and bears witness to a company set to continue on a path of success in providing high-value products to a discerning clientele. The new store was created by architect Sir Norman Foster, with an interior by historic-house designer David Mlinaric. Foster's great glass atrium leads to an emporium created from five 18th-century houses that now house Asprey's own-label and designer ready-to-wear, shoes, fashion accessories, silver, leather goods and trademark jewelry line. The silver room is complete with a recovered 18th-century fireplace.

ART DECO MASTERPIECE
12 Claridge's
55 Brook Street

The august five-star hotel started out as elite as it remains, being designed to accommodate foreign royalty and nobility 'with the discretion of a private house'. Under the direction of celebrity chef Gordon Ramsay, the restaurant, serving principally New French with exceptionally well-orchestrated service in a lush Art Déco setting, has caused a ripple of excitement in the world of haute cuisine, and is often booked weeks in advance. However, the experience of having a cocktail at the lovely Déco bar is worth a visit on its own, or drop in post-dinner to the Fumoir, an elegant cigar-smoker's paradise.

HIGH-STYLE JAPANESE
13 Umu

OLD AND RELIABLE
14 The Guinea
30 Bruton Place

Bruton Place is a quaint little mews off moneyed Berkeley Square, and the Guinea, tucked away down the mews, is a reminder of days past, before the looming buildings surrounding the square were built. The pub, dating back to the 15th century, has a modern restaurant addition that is famous for its classic grills. The small, dark, atmospheric bar is loved by high-flying locals and lucky wanderers alike for its Young's brews and its award-winning steak-and-kidney pies and fine cuts of beef. If the glittering modernity of Mayfair becomes too much, the Guinea is a welcome old-world refuge from the haute cuisine and couture but not from high standards.

THE ARTISAN'S ART
15 Rupert Sanderson
33 Bruton Place

Rupert Sanderson has been quietly making waves in the fashion world, being described in *Vogue* as 'years ahead of his generation'. After training at Cordwainers College, and apprenticing at John Lobb (p. 162), he rode a motorbike around Italy visiting shoe factories, and produced collections for Sergio Rossi and Bruno Magli. His lean, sexy designs are available at various outlets worldwide, but this own-label shop only opened in October 2004. Looking to bring the worlds of fashion and art together, Sanderson wants his premises to have something of the quality of an art gallery about it. To this end it features furnishings from the reclamation specialists Retrouvius, which are for sale. But it is Sanderson's shoes that take centre stage, objects, he says, 'of high craft' such as the dance-hall inspired line for winter 2004.

COLOURFUL CHARACTER
16 Matthew Williamson
28 Bruton Street

Nearly next door to fellow British fashion designer Stella McCartney's own designer shop but a world away in terms of style and approach, Matthew Williamson's flagship store is marked by the hot pink signage on the outside and streaks of bright colour enlivening the cool, white space within. Since launching his debut collection 'Electric Angels' in 1997, which featured bias-cut dresses and separates in tangerine, magenta and fuchsia, he has become known for his sexy, sweeping designs in bold hues. Star clients include Madonna, Sarah Jessica Parker, Gwyneth Paltrow and Kate Moss. The store, which opened in 2004, features ready-to-wear separates as well as products from Williamson's 'lifestyle' range, including candles, the eau de parfum 'Incense' (produced with Lyn Harris, see p. 23) and soon his new signature fragrance.

STAR QUALITY FASHION
17 Stella McCartney

The joining of J.J. Fox and Robert Lewis represents the marriage of two historic tobacco houses. Christopher Lewis set up his shop in 1787, and the first Havana cigars imported to England were sold by his company in 1830. James John Fox began as a tobacco trader in Dublin in the 1870s (his company still holds a royal warrant) and in 1997 launched its own brand of cigars using 100% pure tobacco from Valdrych in the Dominican Republic. In addition to being able to sit in Winston Churchill's favourite chair, aficionados can visit the Fox Museum, located on the shop's ground floor, and trawl through centuries of cigar memorabilia.

Of the several arcades built during the early 19th century, the most famous and longest is the Burlington Arcade (1819). Today, some 70 high-quality shops, many of which are independent, offer a range of clothes, leather goods and jewelry. The smaller Royal Arcade includes a Marti Guixi–designed Camper store, while Princes and Piccadilly Arcades feature menswear.

For the past 17 years, the diminutive premises on Brewer Street has been owned and run by lefty husband-and-wife team, Lauren and Keith Milsom. They stock an extensive range of products, from their acclaimed left-handed scissors to garden tools, kitchen gadgets and clocks that move anti-clockwise. A priceless source for practical items and gifts, and most of the innovative and useful accessories can be tested in store.

Michael Faraday was one of the most famous scientists of his time, conducting groundbreaking research and staging public displays of his discoveries. His inventions, including the electric motor, transformer and generator, have shaped modern life. It was at the Royal Institution, where he spent most of his life, that Faraday made his hugely significant findings. Today the institution houses a tribute to his work in a reconstruction of his lab and in a collection of his original devices for electro-magnetic rotation and induction, the principles behind all current electricity-generating power stations, and a fascinating array of scientific and personal instruments.

Something of an enigma among the tourist-laden streets of Covent Garden, J Sheekey has the high-powered provenance of being under the guidance of the founders of Le Caprice and the Ivy, along with a plain and simple approach that puts quality above frills. So while the décor is plainly pleasant, there is a sense of understated glamour here, as the clientele include theatre producers, directors and actors. More importantly, this just might be the freshest seafood to be served in central London. And whether you go for caviar and lobster, scallops and black pudding, fish cakes or good old fish and chips, it's doubtful you'll be disappointed.

The worn blue awning of the Vintage House shields a veritable *Wunderkammer* of malt whisky, worth a pilgrimage for the connoisseur. On rows of boxed shelves, wines, other liquors and cigars share space with sought-after whiskies. Malts from every region and age include special bottlings and collector's decanters. If the thought of lugging a bottle back on the plane seems too risky, you'll just have to drink it before you leave.

The maze of small, mostly pedestrianized streets behind Regent Street holds everything from chain boutiques to street-market chic. Newburgh Street is home to the funkier European version of the US workwear-maker Carhartt. The Dispensary sells a range of street-style designer labels; across the way is Jess James, featuring jewelry by young makers. Cinch features a high-tech-looking premises originally by Dutch design collective Droog.

This small, unpublike bar is a Soho standby. Though it serves beer only by the half-pint, encouraging the consumption of wine instead, it is often too crowded to move your elbows in the late-week evenings and amicably full the rest of the time. Legend has it that this was a hangout of London members of the French resistance and, sitting as it does, surrounded by traditional old pubs and trendy new cafés, it retains the aura of stubborn pride, much like its home country. Delightfully shabby, it has more character in one scratched wine glass than most of the new places put together. The upstairs restaurant is intimate and off beat but the food varies with the chef.

36 The Pineal Eye

49 Broadwick Street

It's the eye-like structure that some lizards have to detect changes in light. Combining cutting-edge fashion with avant-garde art, this retail version, established by Yuko Yabiku in 1998 responds to new talent in much the same way, changing with every innovation. Changeable as it is, Pineal Eye has been a consistent source for new British and international talents. Exhibitions of fashion and fine art are carried simultaneously with collections handpicked by Yabiku from among the most cutting-edge and newly emerging designers. Together with the artful shop design, the unique selection of work provides an illuminating glimpse into the heart of the edgier London fashion scene.

LONDON STYLE VIA JAPAN

37 Designworks

42–44 Broadwick Street

Who better to re-create classic British clothes with a modern street-smart twist than a Japanese company dedicated to 'New-Brit style'. With the number of Japanese designers dominating the fashion scene even in London, and with the country's reputed fondness for traditional British goods, it is perhaps not surprising that the firm Abahouse has focused on remaking English favourites. The corduroy jacket, the great coat, the Macintosh, they're all here, with a slightly more tailored line, subtle detailing, luxurious fabrics. Last year the design concept moved West, to an American frontier-inspired line that mixes rugged with refined. With the likes of Jude Law and Ewan McGregor as regular customers, Designworks looks to be setting a few trends of its own.

A CLASSIC REBORN

38 Red Fort

142

LITERARY LAIR

39 Hazlitt's

114

STYLISH MICRO-HOTEL

40 West Street

126

41 Ronnie Scott's

47 Frith Street

There are many jazz venues in London, but, set in the heart of Soho's lively nightscape, Ronnie Scott's attracts the biggest international talents. Scott, himself a saxophonist, opened his first club in 1959 with his partner, Pete King, and he was recognized by the Queen in 1981 for his 'services to jazz'. Over the years, the club has featured the very best, Zoot Sims, Stan Getz, Ben Webster, Bill Evans, to name a few. Scott's name is synonymous with jazz in London and abroad, as is the much-revered Frith Street venue, which keeps to the well-loved arrangement of small cocktail tables, dim lighting and low murmurs – all in deference to the artistry of the stage.

VAST COLLECTION OF VINTAGE

42 Rokit

42 Shelton Street

Rokit started trading among the Bohemian streets of Camden in 1982. Now the growing taste for vintage amongst those who like their shops tidy and the merchandise pressed rather than stacked in rumpled piles has brought Rokit into the big time. With shops opened in Brick Lane and Brighton and fashion stylists from the likes of *iD*, *Dazed and Confused* and the *Sun* newspaper plundering their racks for photo shoots, Rokit are set to launch their own label. But you will still find that vintage prom dress, Hawaiian print or 1950s' gabardine shirt, as well as classic army-issue items and nearly new denim all looking crisp, and at prices more down-to-earth than you might think.

POETIC LITTLE LUNCHES

43 Poetry Café

22 Betterton Street

There is more poetry to this little café than the parchment-style lampshades with inked verses scrawled across them. This is the café of the London Poetry Society. By day it's a pleasant but unassuming little café – away from the madding crowd coursing through Covent Garden's nearby pedestrian zones – where light and inexpensive vegetarian lunches are served. There's plenty of coffee and tea, as well as a full bar. At night it becomes the venue for poetry readings, workshops and music. Tuesday nights feature open-mike poetry; on Saturday evenings, it's poetry and jazz.

44 Amphitheatre Café and Restaurant

Royal Opera House, Covent Garden

The Royal Opera House was extended to an acclaimed design to enlarge its facilities and to incorporate it into Covent Garden Piazza in 1999. The centrepiece of the renovation is a soaring, arched-glass atrium that provides glittering bar and restaurant spaces to complement the Royal Opera's internationally celebrated programme. And some of the restored rooms in the original 1858 building offer a particularly grand experience – the Vilar Floral Hall Balconies, which overlook the restored Hall (traditional English menu) and the red-carpeted, neo-classical-style Crush Room (cold meals). But to those simply passing by, the Amphitheatre Restaurant, located on the top floor in a more contemporary, minimalist setting, and the Café are open to the general public from Monday to Saturday for light lunches. Seating on the Terrace, in good weather, affords spectacular views across Covent Garden Piazza. Ticket-holders can book pre-performance, interval and post-performance meals in the various bars as well as the Crush Room and Vilar Balconies.

OFF OF THE MAIN DRAG

45 Floral Street

- Maharishi, no. 19
- Paul Smith, nos 40–44
- Burro, no. 29

Avoid the tourist magnet that has become the Covent Garden Piazza and head for the cobblestoned, pedestrianized Floral Street, where stylish boutiques and funky one-off shops draw insiders and locals. With its more subdued and sophisticated air, the street is the destination for shoppers in search of genuine British goods – Paul Smith's first store is here. Burro is a street-wise label aimed at being 'clean-lined and understated', with screen-printed knits and T-shirts, paint-spattered canvas shoulder bags, all minimal in design and hues. Maharishi is a popular British label, designed by Hardy Blechman, with many deviations on camouflage: combat and cargo trousers, tiger-stripe T-shirts, in a range of colours that would stand out in the city more than the jungle.

FEMININE INDULGENCE

46 The Sanctuary

12 Floral Street

As the name implies, the Sanctuary is an unexpected respite from the immediate activity of Floral Street and a world away. London's most famous women's spa is a shrine to pampering and relaxation. Even the uninitiated might recognize the atrium pool with its rope swing and planted vegetation, as it has featured in numerous photographs and was used by Joan Collins in that infamous masterpiece *The Stud*. A separate exercise pool caters to the fitness-oriented, while the Thai Seating Area encourages nothing more than chatting or reading while cocooned in a plush Sanctuary robe. There are whirlpools, saunas and rooms for facials, massage and aromatherapy, as well as home cooking in the Palm Restaurant, all devoted to the art of de-stressing.

EATING HISTORY

47 Rules

IMPROVING ON A CLASSIC

48 Savoy Grill

The Strand

The Savoy has been an institution of British formal dining for decades, so its 2003 makeover under chef/manager Marcus Wareing (who also runs The Berkeley hotel's acclaimed Pétrus) was always going to cause a bit of a stir among the well-heeled. However, the new kid on this palatial block has proved himself and his business savvy. A bold new interior has not lost its old formality; neither has the service, while the menu has gained a much-needed injection of modernity in both ingredients and pricing. A magnificent whole-roasted Scottish lobster is among the new options, as is king prawn tortellini. But not to worry, the Châteaubriand is still there, only it's been made a little more interesting and a little less expensive than before.

49 Seven Dials/Neal Street/ Monmouth Street

- Coco de Mer, 23 Monmouth Street
- Koh Samui, 65 Monmouth Street
- aquaint, 38 Monmouth Street
- Neal's Yard
- Magma, 8 Earlham Street

This small quarter of narrow, cobblestoned streets and restored buildings has become one of London's most hip shopping areas. Fashion shops and quirky boutiques are interspersed on the streets radiating from the the the circular intersection of seven medieval roads. A short walk along Shorts Gardens takes you to Neal Street, a parade of shops that specialize in weird and wonderful shoes, from trainers and rock-climbing slippers to patent-leather stilettos. Monmouth Street, running north from Seven Dials, and Upper St Martin's Lane, running south, are pockets of design-label boutiques. Coco de Mer, the brainchild of Sam Roddick, daughter of Body Shop entrepreneur and fair-trade pioneer, Anita, offers high-fashion lingerie and erotica. Continuing along the east side of the street, you can stop at the Monmouth Coffee House for a cup of freshly ground dark stuff before heading to Koh Samui, which features a well-chosen selection of top new labels including British designers. Across the road, aquaint, run by designer Ashley Isham, stocks the entire collections of a smaller number of mainly British designers. Neal's Yard, sandwiched between Monmouth Street and Short's Gardens, and entered by way of small alleys, is a centre for organic eating and holistic treatments – Neal's Yard Remedies sells tonics, creams, oils and aromatherapy ingredients all bottled in the distinctive old-style blue glass. Just outside the courtyard, Neal's Yard Dairy is full of gorgeously pungent cheese. Magma is London's leading store for graphics, design and architecture publications, from local rags to obscure imports.

CULTURAL REAWAKENING
50 Somerset House
Strand

- Courtauld Galleries
- The Admiralty
- Riverside Terrace

With an ambitious plan of refurbishment that began in 1997, Somerset House, formerly the forbidding offices of the Inland Revenue, is now home to several art galleries, including one of the country's greatest private art collections, a fine restaurant, terrace dining and lively courtyard fountains designed by architects Jeremy Dixon and Edward Jones. Samuel Courtauld's vast personal collection of Western art was moved to Somerset House, one of England's finest 18th-century buildings, in 1990. World famous Old Master, Renaissance, Impressionist and Post-Impressionist paintings are displayed over three floors. The Gilbert collection of European gold and silver and the Hermitage Rooms are also open for public viewing. Dine in the funky-clubby Admiralty (the name is a reference to the naval offices that used to be based here) established by restaurateur Oliver Peyton (see Inn the Park, p. 149). While the décor, by architect Andrew Martin and designer Solange Azagury-Partridge (see p. 171), is an intriguing mix of traditional and modern British, the food is regional French. Outside, the Riverside Terrace was opened after over 100 years of neglect, and you can enjoy a drink or a meal beneath flowering umbrellas overlooking the Thames. In winter, the courtyard is taken over by an outdoor ice rink.

QUIET AND CLUBBY
51 Adam Street
135

DRIPPING WITH HISTORY
52 Gordon's Wine Bar
151

CELEBRATING THE AVANT-GARDE
53 Institute of Contemporary Arts
The Mall

On the grand route that is The Mall, one of London's few processional avenues, the ICA sits discreetly almost hidden beneath the canopy of chestnut trees that line the way. Here in the genteel surroundings of Nash House, built by John Nash in a clean, neo-classical style in the 1830s, are some of London's most progressive artistic happenings. Exhibitions, talks and performances take place, addressing the newest movements and innovators in the art world. The ICA is also a premier venue for global cinema, as well as hosting DJ-piloted 'club nights'. The ICA bar is a groovy drinking spot that stays open until 1 am.

BUCOLIC BANQUET
54 Inn the Park
149

INDIAN NIGHTS
55 Cinnamon Club
139

Marylebone
Fitzrovia
Bloomsbury
Holborn

CAMDEN
TOWN

PRIMROSE
HILL

Prince Albert Road

Outer Circle

London
Zoo

Delancey St.

Camden High Street

MORNINGTON
CRESCENT

KING'S
CROSS

Pancras Road

KING'S
CROSS
ST PANCRAS

Regent's Park

Eversholt Street

Albany Street

British
Library

Euston Road

CLERKENWELL

Outer Circle

Park Road

Hampstead Road

EUSTON

Queen
Mary's
Gardens

Outer Circle

EUSTON
SQUARE

Woburn Place

Coram's
Fields

Gray's Inn Road

Park
Square
Gardens

Euston Road

WARREN
STREET

RUSSELL
SQUARE

Guilford Street

Roger St.

Rossmore Road

Church Street

1

Lisson Grove

MARYLEBONE

BAKER
STREET

Madame
Tussauds

Marylebone Road

REGENT'S
PARK

GREAT
PORTLAND
STREET

Gower Street

BLOOMSBURY

Southampton Row

Theobalds Road

27

Clerkenwell Rd

Chiltern Street

Paddington St

Marylebone High St.

Harley Street

Portland Place

Great Portland St.

Chenies Street

14

Goodge Street

GOODGE
STREET

Tottenham Court Road

Russell
Square

British
Museum

Bedford Square

Montague
Place

Bloomsbury
Square

Gray's Inn Rd

HATTON GARDEN

CHANCERY
LANE

22 23

Chapel St

Old Marylebone Rd

Baker Street

2   3

Wimpole Street

8

Great Portland St

9

15

Cleveland Street

FITZROVIA

7

6

Mortimer Street

17

Russell Street

Great

New Oxford St

CHANCERY
LANE

High Holborn

21

Gloucester Place

4

5

Wigmore Street

10
11

12

13

16

18   19

Percy St

Rathbone Pl

24

25

26

High Holborn

HOLBORN

Lincoln's
Inn Fields

20

Kingsway

Fetter Lane

Edgware Road

MARYLEBONE

Oxford Street

OXFORD
CIRCUS

Oxford Street

TOTTENHAM
COURT
ROAD

St Giles High St.

Seymour St.

MARBLE ARCH

BOND
STREET

SOHO

Aldwych

MAYFAIR

Approximate scale

1 kilometre

1/2 mile

Marylebone, the area defined roughly by Oxford Street in the south and the Euston and Marylebone Road in the north, is a curious mixture of Edwardian proportions, commercial enterprise, apartment living and discreet stylishness. At the western edge is Marylebone High Street, which, somewhat to the dismay of its loyal inhabitants, has in recent years become one of London's premier gastronomic destinations, with a supporting cast of high-quality shops and design stores. Not far in distance but worlds away from nearby Madame Tussaud's is Chiltern Street, a little-known street with a quirky collection of fine shops. Farther north, past Marylebone Road, is Church Street and Alfie's antiques market, home to a host of antiques dealers well off the beaten track.

Fitzrovia, to the east, is a maze of small and one-way streets inhabited by advertising agencies (like M C Saatchi), engineers (Ove Arup, Buro Happold) and furniture showrooms, making it a hotbed of high design. It gets its name from lovely Fitzroy Square, designed on two sides by the neo-classicist Adam brothers in the 1790s. The quarter also has older creative associations, but more of the starving-artist sort. Atmospheric pubs that were once the haunts of humble writers (T. S. Eliot drank at the Fitzroy Tavern, for example) and artists retain their shabby chic, while others have cleaned house entirely, in favour of cutting-edge media houses and restaurants with seductive interiors by top designers that give nighttime pursuits an infusion of glamour.

Moving east again, on the other side of Tottenham Court Road, the London moderns take hold in the form of the Bloomsbury set, who made this area the centre of literary modernism. Home to University College, the British Museum and, until the late 1990s, the British Library (now in a Scandinavian-inspired building on Euston Road), Bloomsbury retains the aura of a literary and academic enclave, despite the tourist buses that wend their way through the narrow streets. Pleasing squares provide refuge for and reminders of the area's continuing intellectual pursuits.

John Milton, Francis Bacon and Charles Dickens, as well as Dickens's character Pip, all lived for a time in the place known as Holborn, a somewhat transitional area between the old London of the City and the later developments west. The Inns of Court are located here, with their fine buildings and lush enclosed green spaces, as is the former journalists' mecca, Fleet Street, and the wide avenue of the Strand. The best of Holborn is in the isolated historic gems — London's oldest Catholic church and its neighbouring tavern, an eccentric architect's historic house-museum and the underground vaults now used by dealers in silver.

ART DECO EXTRAORDINAIRE

1 **Gallery 1930/Susie Cooper Ceramics**

175

INSTRUMENTS OF PLEASURE

2 **Chiltern Street**

- Gary Anderson, no. 36
- Melbo Couture, no. 39
- Howarth Woodwind Specialists, nos 31–35
- London Harpsichord Centre, no. 14
- Caroline Groves, no. 37
- Philip Somerville, no. 38

Running one street parallel to Baker Street, Chiltern Street is a delightful row of quirky shopfronts below Dorset Street with a curious orientation towards wedding fashion and musicians; many of the latter come from the Royal Academy of Music nearby. For the groom-to-be, Gary Anderson creates fine bespoke formalwear, while the perfect wedding shoes can be sourced (or made) at Melbo Couture. Musicians should stop in at Howarth Woodwind Specialists and the London Harpsichord Centre. Newcomer to an old, traditional space, shoe designer Caroline Groves has taken over the Savva shoe workshop and storefront, which was established in 1934. Groves has added her own unique look to their footwear while retaining a commitment to quality and personal service. Next door Philip Somerville hats add the final touch to the wedding wear available in several of the neighbouring boutiques.

A WORLD OF TRAVEL BOOKS

3 **Daunt Books**
83–84 Marylebone High Street

Marylebone High Street has a surprisingly pleasant village atmosphere, but Daunt Books would be enough to lure travellers here even without the surrounding shops and cafés. There are many who consider its Edwardian rooms to house London's most beautiful bookshop. The *pièce de résistance* in both character and design is its foreign section, where James Daunt features not only guides and maps but histories, fiction and cookery titles – all helpfully arranged by country. The travel section is housed in the beautiful atrium space with a gallery running along both walls.

GRAND TOWNHOUSE MUSEUM

4 **Wallace Collection**
Manchester Square

The often-overlooked Wallace Collection is a privately amassed assembly of art bequeathed to the nation by Lady Wallace, widow of Sir Richard Wallace, in 1897. Among the treasures housed in the grand period rooms of this late 18th-century townhouse are a renowned collection of French 18th-century pictures, porcelain and furniture, some fine 17th-century paintings and a rather intriguing armoury. A superb glassed atrium was added in the 2000 renovation and expansion, designed by Rick Mather, providing an ideal place for lunch, tea or a glass of wine.

HAND-SPUN HOME DÉCOR

5 **Mint**
70 Wigmore Street

Mint 'is ethnic, tribal, old and new, solid and pure, handmade ordinary everyday objects presented as extraordinary', according to shopowner Lina Kalafani. This wilfully 'eclectic' range of furnishings, textiles and accessories is arranged over two floors of a former wine store and cellar. Next to an old Tibetan chest you might find a piece by Henry Harris, a pair of felt slippers among the glassware, ceramics and pots. As in any good eclectic shop, the selection changes frequently.

OPULENT MEZE

6 **Ozer**
4–5 Langham Place

Langham Place is the northern continuation of Regent Street, which features a number of chain-food outlets and one plush, ruby-red pocket that is Ozer, a nouvelle Turkish-Mediterranean restaurant that wins rave reviews for its lush interior and innovative approach to traditional Turkish cuisine. Chef Huseyin Ozer offers the conventional mixed meze dish as a delectable *belle présentation*, a popular favourite of lunching BBC executives who work along the street. Ozer offers a striking interior, varied menu and service bound by Ozer's personal guarantee of satisfaction.

PUBLIC HOUSE PLEASANTRIES

7 **Dover Castle**
43 Weymouth Mews

This Georgian pub, tucked down a mews in a quarter of mainly private and ambassadorial residences – and just a stone's throw from the RIBA headquarters – is the perfect place to settle in for a pint. Whether you choose to admire the 1777 interior and wood-panelled dining room, or to join those who spill out into the mews, you will be among the people who live and work here, in a setting visited by few others.

8 Royal Institute of British Architects
66 Portland Place

The Royal Institute of British Architects is housed in a grand 1930s building that includes galleries, meeting rooms, a café and a world-class architecture bookshop. With 30,000 members, it is one of the most influential architecture bodies in the world. Regular exhibitions, lectures and events highlight new architecture from around the globe. The contemporary first-floor café, recently remodelled by the Conran group, buzzes with figures from the architecture community and nearby embassies and consulates lining Portland Place.

FRENCH CAFÉ
9 Villandry
170 Great Portland Street

Despite their distinctly French affiliations, which includes produce delivered from Paris, the delicatessen and restaurant at Villandry have become something of a Fitzrovia institution. The food shop is a mainstay of many in search of gourmet ingredients, and the dining room boasts rustic French recipes executed with authentic rigour. Should you find yourself in Regent's Park or near Oxford Street, it is a perfect place for a daytime drink or coffee, or a light lunch featuring nicely accented dishes like pan-fried cod and a great wine list.

OF HEARTH AND HOME
10 CVO Firevault
36 Great Titchfield Street

In an area swimming with modern- and contract-furniture showrooms, CVO Firevault is an interior décor store with a difference. Named for the elegant hearth designs on display, it also features an attractive array of objects, clothing and soft furnishings to enjoy around the glowing flames. The real draw, however, is the downstairs café-bar, whose rich ambience cannot be divined from the exterior and has made it an atmospheric hideaway.

THE ENGLISH SAUSAGE REDUX
11 R. K. Stanley's
6 Little Portland Street

Although the interior of patterned concrete blocks was drawn from the work of Frank Lloyd Wright and diner-style red-leatherette booths may have an American flavour, the fare is distinctly British – sausage, mash and beer. What might seem to be a conventional dish, however, is enhanced by international influences, such as sausages infused with Thai or French seasonings and updated with spicy noodles, chips or gravied mash.

SUPERIOR MIXES
12 The Social
 157

IRONICALLY STYLISH ACCOMMODATION
13 The Sanderson
 120

SPOILED FOR GOURMET CHOICE
14 Charlotte Street
- Fino, no. 33
- Pied à Terre, no. 34
- Passione, no. 10
- Bam-Bou, 1 Percy Street
- Rasa Samudra, no. 5

This Fitzrovian throughway has become a hub of high-style international cuisine. Choose from a fine selection of modern tapas-style dishes at Fino or consistently well-prepared haute French cuisine at Pied à Terre, recently renewed after a kitchen fire. Updated and upmarket Italian fare is always on offer at Passione, where chef-proprietor Gennaro Contaldo serves the classics with quality. For French-Vietnamese fusion, Bam-Bou continues to please with spicy additions to traditional dishes. Upstairs, the Lotus Rooms offer cocktails in a cool, elegant Vietnamese atmosphere. Chef Das Sreedharan has made Indian seafood an art at Rasa Samudra, where fish, curry and chilli combinations are pleasantly inventive and well matched.

GRILL AND SPIRITS
15 Roka
37 Charlotte Street

Partner to Zuma in Knightsbridge, Roka has at its heart the robata grill used for a Japanese cuisine that involves searing and roasting handcrafted portions of beef, chicken, pork, fish and vegetables. Seats at the robata bar are first come first served, but tables in the dining area can be reserved. In the more intimate Shochu Lounge downstairs, dark wood and soft chairs and banquettes upholstered in perky Japanese prints provide a sultry atmosphere for sipping Shochu, a vodka-like drink that comes in a variety of flavours, such as lemon, plum and strawberry and is served as an aperitif in rippled glasses.

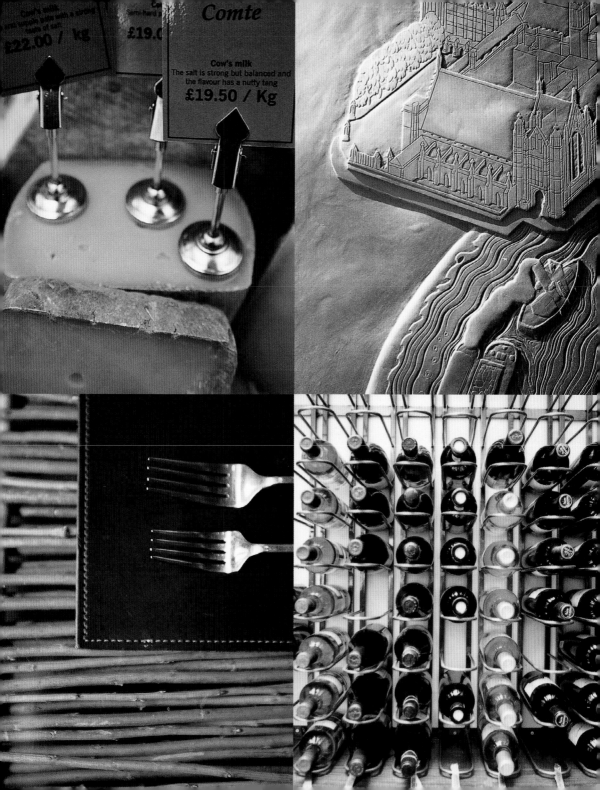

Sushi, sashimi, salads, tempura, rice and noodle dishes are all constructed with just the right amount and range of ingredients.

CLASSIC ENGLISH PIES
16 Newman Arms
23 Rathbone Street

Among London's achingly modern restaurants and gastro pubs, the Newman Arms, set in a quiet side street, is a small, simple, satisfying locale where the best homemade savoury pies are served. Downstairs is a tight but cosy room for drinks, but the upstairs room, with fewer than a dozen tables, serves a straightforward menu of pie and puddings – steak and kidney, chicken and broccoli, ham and leek – served with friendliness and rather large puff-pastry tops. They only serve lunch, however, and you'll need a good hunger – especially if you opt for the sticky-toffee pudding.

BRITISH MODERN
17 Target Gallery
7 Windmill Street

This unassuming gallery off Goodge Street near Tottenham Court Road has been quietly gaining a reputation for its collection of modernist furniture, ceramics, textiles and glass. The focus is on British makers such as Robin Day, Frank Guille, William Plunkett and John and Sylvia Reid, but there is also a selection of Italian, Scandinavian and French designers, graphics and Pop Art posters, jewelry by Anton Michelsen, Georg Jensen and Hans Hansen, and a host of other items from the 1930s to the 1970s.

BRITISH ARTS AND CRAFTS
18 Contemporary Applied Arts
2 Percy Street

Founded in 1948 in the spirit of the turn-of-the-century Arts and Crafts movement, Contemporary Applied Arts is the largest private gallery in Britain for contemporary crafts, with a large regular stock and exhibitions of all media: fine and costume jewelry, metalwork, ceramics, wood, textiles, furniture, glass, bookbinding and paper. Works can be bought on site or commissioned from the hundreds of makers on their books.

EASTERN BEAUTY
19 Hakkasan
133

AN INDOOR FOLLY
20 Sir John Soane's Museum
13 Lincoln's Inn Fields

Sir John Soane (1753–1837) was a distinguished architect (most notably of the Bank of England) and art and artefact collector. During his lifetime he amassed antiquities, archaeological fragments, architectural prints and drawings. The house was completed in 1824, and upon his death in 1837, Soane bequeathed the house and its contents to trustees with the mandate that it be preserved in its original condition. A visit to the Soane, a jewel-box of delights and surprises is a trip into one man's obsessions and love. If that weren't enough, there are paintings by Canaletto, Turner and Reynolds, and two series by Hogarth. A particular treat is the first Tuesday of each month, when the museum is open in the evening and rooms are lit with candles.

SECRETED SILVERWARE
21 London Silver Vaults
53–64 Chancery Lane

The world's largest collection of antique silver is housed in 37 shops beneath a plain building in what were once the strongrooms for the safe deposit of valuables for wealthy Londoners. From 1867, the vaults were guarded night and day, as they are today, and there has never been a robbery. Since 1953, the vaults have been occupied by dealers, and it has been *the* place to find silver at near dealers' prices. Even if you don't require any Georgian silver plate or Victorian candlesticks, a descent into this quirky arcade is well worth the trip – few locals even know of its existence.

SANCTUARY OF AGES
22 St Etheldreda
Ely Place

One of London's most intimate and atmospheric churches, St Etheldreda was built in about 1293 and is the oldest surviving Catholic church the city. In the early 17th century it was a place of refuge for persecuted Catholics. Much of the church was damaged in the Second World War, not, however, the walls of the undercroft, once used as a tavern, which contain Roman foundations dating from the third century.

ANOINTED PUB
23 Ye Olde Mitre Tavern
152

SIR JOHN SOANE'S
MUSEUM
Open Tuesday-Saturday
10 AM ~ 5 PM
(6-9pm on the first Tuesday
of the month)
ADMISSION FREE
Groups must book in advance
TEL: 0171 405-2107
Lecture tour on Saturday 2:30

LAMBS CONDUIT
STREET   WC1

THE
FAMOUS
PIE ROOM
12-3 P.M. MON-FRI; 6-9PM MON-FRI
PUB OPENING TIMES: 11·30AM-11PM.
HOME BAKED
PUDDINGS
AND
PIES
BOOKING ADVISABLE
020 7636 1127

24 Cornelissen & Son

105 Great Russell Street

It looks like an old apothecary's shop with black-painted wood drawers holding all sorts of interesting titbits and antique cabinetry stuffed with paint pots and tubes, brushes, papers and other specialist artists' necessities. Established in 1855, Cornelissen and Son have an international reputation as 'artists' colourmen' that provided them with a busy mail-order business long before the internet made their stock available worldwide in 2004. However, a visit to the traditional Victorian-era shop, which Cornelissen acquired in 1980, is an altogether more fascinating experience than scrolling through their products online. Here, a stone's throw from the British Museum, professionals and amateurs convene, looking for rare pigments, special varieties of gum, books of gold leaf or one of the thousands of shades of pastel. The more specialized the request, the better the staff like to fill it.

25 James Smith and Son Umbrellas

55 New Oxford Street

The exterior of this shop makes such a wonderful backdrop for photographs that too many people forget to go inside. Yet James Smith and Son really is the ultimate in umbrellas and walking sticks. The first Smith set up shop in 1830 and his son moved the business to these premises in 1857, which has been maintained ever since by the Smith family. With the same fittings specially created for it by its own Victorian craftsmen, this was the first company to make use of the Fox steel frame, which distinguishes the Smith and Son umbrella as the finest in the sky. The company continues to produce walking sticks, though they may be more at home in the country than the city. Umbrellas range from those created for ceremonial purposes to the everyday, in either solid sombre tones or explosions of vivid colour, and all are working symbols of an era of fine workmanship – and a necessary London accessory.

26 Joie
10 Museum Street

Just down the street from the British Museum, in an unlikely spot next to an ancient greasy spoon and around the corner from hip dance club The End is Joie, which sells its own line of delicate, diaphanous designs. Its one-off collections have long appealed, in a quiet way, to a discerning fashion crowd, who perhaps catch a glimpse of the collection before hitting the dance floor. The small shop, seemingly overgrown by forest vegetation, is a suitable background to dresses, skirts and tops that are playful and contemporary.

PUBLIC HOUSE MODERNE
27 The Duke (of York)
7 Roger Street

The 1940s are alive and well in this hidden little pub down a narrow street off Gray's Inn Road. You'll certainly need to know it's there, but once you do, you'll be drawn by the warm mustard-yellow walls, the red lacquered piano in the corner, the changing selection of pictures. The back lounge bar is the most captivating, with wood-backed banquettes that give it the feeling of an old railway café or speakeasy. Pubs of genuine interest from periods after the Victorian age are rare in London, so this pre-modern pub has a slightly off-beat ambiance, though the choice of beers and fresh, modern cuisine will appeal to most.

Clerkenwell
Islington
King's Cross

The areas north of Smithfield – or 'smooth field' as it was once known – Clerkenwell, King's Cross and Islington, amply demonstrate how new life and vitality can emerge out of a dense urban fabric. On the border of the City, acting as a kind of fulcrum between it and its lively northern neighbours, is the church of St Bartholomew the Great, which stands proud amid all the surrounding redevelopment. Smithfield Market, a place for cattle and horse trading since the Middle Ages (today a meat market) signals a modern transition with nightclub-goers herding into the Victorian warehouse buildings turned dance venues.

Conversions continue in Clerkenwell, north, a district once known for its light industrial buildings and lively printing presses, many of which have become stylish lofts. Animated by journalists from *The Guardian* newspaper and a number of internationally renowned architectural figures, such as Zaha Hadid, Clerkenwell embodies that typical London alchemy in which the old world and new ideas fuse into something exciting and unexpected.

Islington, northward again, is another area of successful regeneration. In the 19th century it was one of London's first suburbs, with some of the most unusual and intimate residential squares. Its central-fringe location made it attractive to artists, writers and City bankers, who poured in during the 1970s to refurbish and restore neglected buildings. Today it is one of the most lively and creative of London's villages and still marked by patrician elegance. And although Upper Street, the neighbourhood's main thoroughfare, is lined by chain stores, street markets, such as Camden Passage (p. 81), independent boutiques and bars ensure the area maintains its street style. Islington is also enlivened by the highest density of theatres in London, making it a popular stomping ground for thespians and theatre mavens.

King's Cross, which was known until very recently as just a train station, is now considered a neighbourhood in its own right. The imminent arrival of the high-speed rail link to Paris (a mere 2.5-hour ride away) has spawned numerous loft developments coinciding with a profusion of groovy bars and shops. Some people have appreciated the neighbourhood's off-beat feel for years: arch-minimalist John Pawson and design wunderkind Thomas Heatherwick have their studios here, as do the corporate-branding gurus at Wolff Olins. Even though these areas are just outside the ring of tourist attractions (but within an easy walk of the British Library), they have a strong local character that is enriched by the creative and literary people who live there.

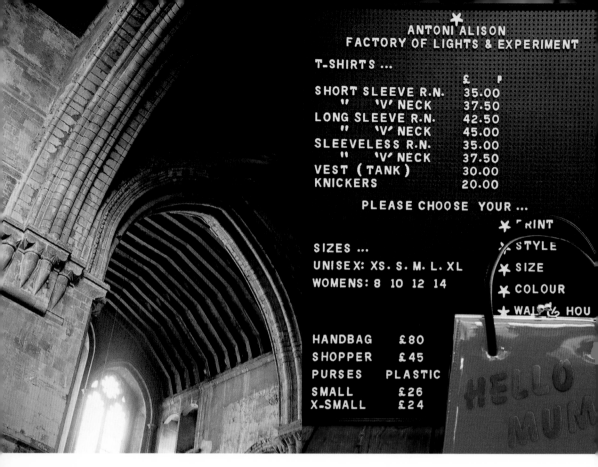

ANTONI ALISON
FACTORY OF LIGHTS & EXPERIMENT

T-SHIRTS ...   £   p
SHORT SLEEVE R.N.   35.00
     "   'V' NECK   37.50
LONG SLEEVE R.N.   42.50
     "   'V' NECK   45.00
SLEEVELESS R.N.   35.00
     "   'V' NECK   37.50
VEST (TANK)   30.00
KNICKERS   20.00

PLEASE CHOOSE YOUR ...
                              ✳ PRINT
SIZES ...   ✳ STYLE
UNISEX: XS. S. M. L. XL   ✳ SIZE
WOMENS: 8 10 12 14   ✳ COLOUR
                              ✳ WAIST & HOU

HANDBAG   £80
SHOPPER   £45
PURSES   PLASTIC
SMALL   £26
X-SMALL   £24

HELLO MUM

CHARMED CHAPEL

1   St Bartholomew the Great

West Smithfield

In a lovely preserved corner of narrow streets lined with traditional-style pubs and shops just across from Smithfield Market lies this small, often overlooked church, the only vestige of the priory founded along with the old St Bartholomew's Hospital (now St Bart's) in 1123 by the Augustinian Rahere. Sections of the church have been rebuilt – the Lady Chapel in 1336, central tower in 1628 – and it fell into disrepair until it was restored in the late 19th century. Today it has an intimate, spare interior, an oasis in a bustling city centre, a little illumination of medieval London.

BOUDOIR-CHIC HOTEL

2   The Rookery

118

'FACTORY OF LIGHTS AND EXPERIMENT'

3   Antoni & Alison

43 Rosebery Avenue

Known for their quirky and wry photographic-print T-shirts and whimsical accessories, Antoni Burakowski and Alison Roberts gained notoriety with their refreshingly humorous catwalk shows. Now their energy and bravado have been channelled into creating a full-blown collection of street-savvy ready-to-wear pieces, including knitwear, dresses, skirts and trousers.

'NOSE TO TAIL DINING'

4   St John

144

URBAN INN

5   The Zetter

112

CREATIVE CENTRE

6 Clerkenwell Green

- Lesley Craze Gallery, nos 33–35A
- Marx Memorial Library, no. 37A

Clerkenwell has become a mecca for young designers of all media and gradually also yielded to patches of gentrification. At the heart of the revitalization is Clerkenwell Green, a pleasant Georgian square landmarked by the spire of St James's church, which features shops selling brilliant original creations: the Lesley Craze Gallery has established itself as a showcase for new designs in precious jewelry and carries pieces by over 100 British-based artists. There are also textiles and woven creations by local artisans. For an antidote to any shopping extravagances, visit the Marx Memorial Library, home to waves of revolutionaries, with a subscription library specializing in socialist literature, which was opened in response to the Nazi book-burnings.

MARKET FRESH

7 Smiths of Smithfield

67–77 Charterhouse Street

Smiths sits facing the old cattle market, Smithfields, and if you were expecting beef then you won't be disappointed. John Torode (formerly of Quaglino's and Mezzo) has embraced traditional British food and spruced it up with Thai and Italian touches. He began by sourcing rare and organic breeds in Britain for his meat and poultry dishes, and he buys organic produce whenever possible. The venue, a former meatpacking warehouse, is historic, with a large, informal ground floor filled with refectory tables that serves breakfast all day long. On the first floor is a red-leather-boothed cocktail bar to lubricate the way to the second-floor dining room, an informal seated service. The Top Floor is the showpiece for Torode's rare and organic breed dishes: Gloucester Old Spot pork fillet with bok choi, crab ravioli and Thai broth; or Welsh black sirloin (aged 26 days).

Morag Myerscough invites you to visit her at home, wander around her kitchen, sit on a sofa and perhaps buy a design object or two. In Her House, a Victorian townhouse, which is actually where she lives, Myerscough presents a range of contemporary design objects from a number of British makers. Artworks, furniture, ceramics and textiles are arranged much as they would be in the home – admittedly a particularly style-conscious home. A patron of emerging artists and designers, Myerscough also helps develop and produce new products under the 'her house' brand. In 2003 she collaborated with designer Luke Morgan to create their successful range of 'shoe plates'. These might be set out on the glass dining table overhung with a lamp by Myerscough and Morgan. And don't forget to visit the bathroom, where a claw-footed tub keeps company with a range of tempting oil paintings.

The exterior of the Quality Chop House, around the corner from Exmouth Market in the media-dominated Farringdon Road, looks like it has been around for centuries and that the menu hasn't changed much in that time. In fact, it has been around since the 19th century but in its present incarnation, thankfully for diners at least, for about a dozen years. Though 'progressive working-class caterer' is etched on the front window, and paper napkins, jarred condiments and a plain menu suggest a certain humility, the dishes, as prepared by chef Charles Fontaine, are upwardly mobile and cater to the journalists, bankers, creatives and locals alike. Classic dishes, such as jellied eels and grilled lobster, are served in a classic setting of high-backed settle benches. It's not luxurious, but it is quality.

On Monday mornings market stalls sell woven bags, gourmet sausages, cheeses, olives, oils. But every other day this semi-pedestrianized street is brimming with new establishments sitting next to the few remaining local shops. Moro caused a spicy sensation when it opened and continues to please with its inspired North African dishes and Spanish tapas, served by Sam and Sam Clark. Since then, the arrival of the Exmouth Grill has added another quality option to casual lunch and dinner, while Medcalf (occupying the former butcher's shop), with its dark, rustic-chic interior, serves hearty dishes with French overtones that are reliably good. The downstairs Martini Lounge at the Dollar Bar is an experience in kitschy bling and well-mixed cocktails. For the craft connoisseur, EC One sells jewelry from over 40 mostly British designers, as well as a range of bespoke wedding and engagement rings designed by partner and goldsmith Jos Skeates. Japanese-born Takako Copeland and her husband, Matthew, decided to set up Family Tree with a group of friends who considered themselves a 'family' of designers. Takako mans the store that displays her own, handcrafted jewelry pieces that use precious metals, semi-precious stones and Swarovski crystals. However, the jewelry competes for attention with handmade shoes, belts and scarves that all have a distinctly bespoke quality. So, too, do the handmade soaps and tiny boxes for 'transporting valuable insects'.

THE ORIGINAL GASTRO-PUB
11 The Eagle

138

12 Fish Shop on St John Street

360–62 St John Street

The owners of the former Upper Street Fish Shop whose departure was much-lamented by Islingtonians several years ago have gone one better by opening a more upscale version of their beloved fish and chips restaurant. The Fish Shop serves fish and shellfish fresh for the day from Billingsgate Market in mostly unadulterated forms that leave the creativity in the chef's selection. The standard battered plaice, cod and haddock are still on the menu, as are things like Cornish crab (served half or whole), rock oysters, fresh langoustines and native lobster. The focus is on the variety of fresh fish simply pan fried, seared or cooked in batter (or egg and matzo).

DANCE ELECTRIC

13 Sadler's Wells

Rosebery Avenue

On the site of a well believed to have medicinal properties, Thomas Sadler built a 'musick' house in 1683 to provide a variety of entertainments for the many visitors looking to take the cure, and there has been some kind of theatre on the site ever since. Today Sadler's Wells is primarily a theatre of modern dance, presenting an international and highly regarded programme. The new building, completed in 1998, has a modern appeal and facilities, as well as three bars, a café and exhibition area. Recent performances have ranged from choreographer Pina Bausch's carnation-filled *Nelka* to several more classic productions by Matthew Bourne and a rollicking run of the London Flamenco Festival in 2005.

WOVEN ARTS

14 Wallace Sewell

24 Lloyd Baker Street (corner of Amwell Street)

Harriet Wallace-Jones and Emma Sewell have been weaving together since they graduated from the Royal College of Art in 1990 and their fabrics have been long been sold through Liberty and the Crafts Council in London as well as through select stockists abroad. In late 2003, however, they opened their own shop on the creative mecca of Amwell Street in Clerkenwell. It features the full range of their scarf, throw and cushion collections, which they design on two looms downstairs and then have produced in small quantities at a factory in England. Intricate colourblock and vibrant striped designs are inspired by the Bauhaus and the Colourist painters. Textured weaves in silk, cashmere and mohair for winter and silk, crepe and linen for summer are individual works of art, as the hand-crafted approach endures from conception through dyeing to the detailing.

CONTEMPORARY CRAFTS

15 Crafts Council

44A Pentonville Road

Leading up from King's Cross, Pentonville Road is large, noisy and not particularly friendly to the senses, but the Crafts Council, just around the corner from the Angel tube station at the bottom of Islington's Upper Street, is friendly indeed. Britain's largest crafts gallery holds over 1,200 works in metal, paper, plastic, ceramic, glass, wood, bookbinding and other media in its permanent collection. Set up as an outlet to make crafts accessible to the public in 1972, it has become a major source of support and promotion for craftsmen and -women around the country. Works on display represent a range of new and established makers, as does the gallery shop where craft pieces can be purchased or commissions arranged.

CIVILIZED DRINKING

16 Islington Pubs

- The Crown, 116 Cloudesley Road
- The Draper's Arms, 44 Barnsbury Street
- Duke of Cambridge, 30 St Peter's Street

As increasingly ubiquitous gastro-pubs go, the Crown is an old favourite. Established several years ago on a quiet street away from the traffic and in the heart of the Barnsbury conservation area, it can be relied upon for pleasant food and atmosphere, a clever selection of wines, Hoegaarden blond beer and Czech pilsner Staaropramen on tap. The Draper's Arms has been winning accolades from London pundits and Michelin critics alike for its menu; but popularity from the locals also comes from the very comfortably, slightly upscale atmosphere that's just as good for a pint or a bottle of wine. Meanwhile, in the genteel Canonbury neighbourhood of Islington, Geetie Singh and Esther Boulton's revamped corner pub continues to attract organic foodies from all over the city.

WINE IN TRANSIT

17 Smithy's

153

18 Gagosian Gallery

6–24 Britannia Street

The Gagosian Gallery, one of the contemporary art world's hottest tickets with galleries in New York on Madison Avenue and in Chelsea, has made a bold move that some believe will bring further regeneration to King's Cross. Gagosian is the first major gallery in the upcoming area, with a deftly illuminated backdrop forged by architects Caruso St John in a former industrial building.

RED-LIGHT ZONE

19 Ruby Lounge

157

SHOES FIT FOR A PRINCESS

20 Joe Tan

98 Caledonian Road

When he first arrived in London, it was to work with fellow Malaysian designer Jimmy Choo. Tan quickly showed his talent and became the shoe designer for Princess Diana among other royalty and celebrity customers. His first solo shop stands out among the regenerating streets of King's Cross with its luxurious swag draperies and bedecked footwear perched regally in the window. He still creates custom-made shoes for members of the elite crowd, but is keen to establish himself for a larger audience with an eye for detailing and personal attention.

ACTORS' FAVOURITE

21 Almeida Theatre

Almeida Street

Since it opened as a performance venue in 1980, the Almeida has become one of the most highly regarded small theatres in London. It formed its own producing company in 1990 under the joint directorship of actors Ian McDiarmid and Jonathan Kent, who quickly became known as the man who brought Hollywood to Islington. A-list talents such as Claire Bloom, Ralph Fiennes, Juliet Binoche and Kevin Spacey (now at the Old Vic, see p. 105) helped the theatre to earn dozens of awards. In 2002 Michael Attenborough was named artistic director, and the refurbished and modernized 1837 building re-opened in 2003 with a full programme, set to please the public and actors alike.

UPWARD MOBILITY

22 Upper Street

- The King's Head, no. 115
- Twenty Twenty-one, no. 274
- Gill Wing Shops, nos 182, 190, 194, 196
- Euphorium Bakery, no. 203
- Stephen Einhorn, no. 210

Despite its over-commercialization, the exceptional aspects that have made Islington a local and international destination – theatres, crafts, antiques, restaurants – are still thriving at points along Upper Street. At the south end is Camden Passage antiques market (see below). The King's Head is an old favourite, a pub-cum-theatre that features everything from solo performances to vaudeville and Irish music. High-design modern furniture and domestic objects are at Twenty Twenty-one (and their showroom off Amwell Street). The family of Gill Wing shops sell cookery items, shoes, quirky accessories and gadgets, menswear and craft-based jewelry. The Euphorium Bakery delights with gourmet bread and pastries. For new Gothic silverworks, Stephen Einhorn produces a whole range of jewelry for men and women.

ANTIQUES EMPIRE

23 Camden Passage Antiques Market

Off Upper Street

- The Mall, 359 Islington High Street
- Frederick's, 106 Camden Passage
- Annie's, 12 Camden Passage
- Tadema Gallery, 10 Charlton Place
- Elk in the Woods, 39 Camden Passage

Revived from the doldrums in the 1960s, Camden Passage is a hive of antiquarian activity on Wednesdays and Saturdays that is almost hidden from the many shoppers who come to the busy Islington Upper Street. The Mall is full of tiny spaces selling everything from antique tiaras and tea services to Art Déco ceramics and wooden sailing ships. Frederick's is an Islington institution featuring a large conservatory and post-hunting luxuries like lobster and beef. In Camden Passage look for Annie's vintage clothing, filled with extravagant beaded flapper dresses and lacey Victorian linens. Tadema has immaculate Art Nouveau, Jugendstil and Arts and Crafts jewelry. Be sure to check out the overflowing rooms of the Pierrepont Row. A recent, welcome addition is Elk in the Woods, a homely and upbeat bar and a restaurant for earthy gourmands. The log-cabin-style décor brightened with low lighting beckons wanderers in from Camden Passage for a drink and a warm chat.

24 Cross Street

- Fandango, no. 50
- Suzy Harper, no. 44
- Canal, no. 42
- Cross Street Gallery, no. 40

A small lane lined with Georgian townhouses between Essex Road and Upper Street and filled with intriguing independent shops and boutiques, Cross Street makes a pleasant detour from the crowds. Fandango offers unexpected mid-century modern treats like 'Sputnik' hanging lamps and Arne Jacobsen chairs. Suzy Harper has wispy dresses and blouses in quality cotton and linen. With its finely woven scarves, shawls, jackets and other textiles made in India to designs conceived in-house, Canal is a visual and textural delight. No. 40 is the Cross Street Gallery, a small space specializing in contemporary paintings and prints by artists such as Bridget Riley.

EDGE CONDITIONS
25 Essex Road

- Get Stuffed, no. 105
- Old Queen's Head, no. 44
- S & M, nos 4–6

Where Upper Street has largely been taken over by large chains, Essex Road running very close by represents the edgier, funkier side of affluent Islington. Historic Essex Road is found in the Old Queen's Head, originally Elizabethan, torn down in 1829 and rebuilt with its original 16th-century plaster ceiling and chimneypiece intact. A quirky favourite is Get Stuffed, a taxidermy shop where you can buy a stuffed lion, wolf, peacock, kangaroo or just about any other animal, as well as the glass case to keep it in. Sausages and mash are English comfort food and the 1950s-style diner S & M is all about a comfortable nostalgia, from the chrome detailing and bright blue formica table tops to the simple menu and coke in a bottle. Choose from a variety of sausages from S & M's own mix to vegetarian versions served with a choice of gravies and sides (mushy peas, bubble and squeak) and daily specials, but leave room for homemade pudding.

BOUTIQUE STYLE
26 Comfort and Joy
109 Essex Road

Anthony Wilson and Ruth Llewellyn, founders of Comfort and Joy, are designers of smart, well-made, original womenswear. The pair opened this shop in 2000 and have attracted a loyal clientele. Featuring Llewellyn's slightly retro designs in high-quality, eye-catching fabrics, along with a range of local designers, Comfort and Joy offers clothing that you will not find on the high street at prices that are not far off what you pay for factory-produced merchandise. Find incredibly reasonable tags for one-off or very limited runs of shirts, dresses, trousers and skirts. Blue Stone, a range created by a Japanese designer, and Lumi, by a Finnish contributor, are just two labels that offer singular pieces. Definitely a destination for those with an eye for fashion discoveries.

ITALIAN FUTURISTS
27 Estorick Collection
39A Canonbury Square

Eric Estorick was an American writer and sociologist who lived in England after the Second World War and, with his wife, Salome Dessau, started collecting 20th-century Italian art. Their lively collection has been featured in museum exhibitions since the 1950s but found its home, in a restored Georgian manor off picturesque Canonbury Square, only in 1998. The collection focuses on Italian Futurist works and figurative art dating from 1890 to the 1950s. Giacomo Balla, Umberto Boccioni, Carlo Carrà, Gino Severini, Luigi Russolo and Ardengo Soffici are all represented, as are Giorgio De Chirico, Amedeo Modigliani, Giorgio Morandi, Mario Sironi and Marino Marini. The small museum also has an art library, café and bookshop.

THE GOOD LIFE STYLE
28 Palette London
21 Canonbury Lane

Palette London is the brainchild of owner/manager Marco Ellis, whose shop is dominated by designer vintage clothing but who claims to adhere to the rule that 'if the item is gorgeous, unusual or superbly designed' whether vintage or modern, he'll consider adding it to his collection. Though he stocks mint condition designer clothing from the 1920s through to the 1980s, including gems by Christian Lacroix, Emilio Pucci, Oscar de la Renta and Comme des Garçons, he insists that the shop is about 'a whole lifestyle concept'. To this end he includes furniture, accessories by Unto this Last (see p. 90), organic bath products and wallpaper, among the mix of vintage and contemporary treasures.

City
Brick Lane
Shoreditch

Old London, the Square Mile, the City — all refer to the original settled area on the Thames, the area once ruled by the Romans, now largely known as the financial district, but still imbued with the mystique of the ages. The 11th-century Tower of London was William the Conqueror's declaration of triumph; St Paul's Cathedral a signal of rebirth after the Great Plague of 1665 and the Great Fire of 1666 and a symbol of strength during the Second World War. The City is rife with history and the characters of history — Spenser and Chaucer were born here and Shakespeare flourished here. Nowhere is the fabric of history more tangible than in the architecture — the oldest, smallest, quirkiest streets matched by the public houses that have stood for centuries are set off by the span of bridges and the profusion of early 18th-century churches. Massive rebuilding after the Second World War wasn't particularly design-conscious, but new life has come to the old city, and buildings once threatened with demolition are being saved by the revitalization of marketplaces.

One of the most successful centres of civic rejuvenation is north of the City in the area known as Shoreditch. Once a wasteland of disused light industrial buildings, it has progressed from arty bohemian village to almost upscale status. Artists still occupy many of the loft spaces, as do galleries and design-label boutiques featuring local talent. Its artistic profile is heightened by the presence of the White Cube gallery on Hoxton Square, which has lost much of its edginess but not its edge. If you're looking for innovation in music, art and fashion before it gets to the high street, it probably starts here.

Farther east, amid the cacophony of sights and smells that is the East End, Brick Lane, where the rag trade, Indian restaurants and odd design experiments converge, is attracting its fair share of creatives. This was once a track used as a route for transporting tiles and bricks during the rebuilding of London after the Great Fire. Spitalfields was an early home to nonconformists, later a Jewish ghetto, then, beginning in the 1960s, a community of largely Bangladeshi immigrants. The area was steeped in their culture, and Brick Lane became synonymous with homestyle curry. But change continues, and both the creative industries and the cuisine have experienced injections of new talent and innovation. The Truman Brewery complex has become a centre for fashion, art and design, while young entrepreneurs have elevated the curry house from its humble origins. On the weekends, Brick Lane has a lively atmosphere, with wonderful food and an ever-changing kaleidoscope of one-off boutiques.

ART NOUVEAU PUB

1 The Blackfriar

CHRISTOPHER WREN CHURCH

2 St Stephen Walbrook

Walbrook Street

There has been a church on this site since before 1096; the previous one, having been built in 1439, burned down in the Great Fire of 1666. Christopher Wren, architect of St Paul's, rebuilt the current St Stephen in 1679 using some methods he would later employ in the great cathedral, including the large central dome, described by one observer as 'a bubble of light'. Although damaged in bombing during the Second World War, it retains its 17th-century features, such as the communion rails, pulpit and font, making for a fascinating glimpse into the mind and career of one of London's greatest architects.

CROOKED LITTLE PUBLIC HOUSE

3 Jamaica Wine House

12 St Michael's Alley

This, London's first coffee house, reeks with history even after a recent refurbishment has propped up sagging timbers. The first building was damaged in the Great Fire but stood long enough to survive the Cornhill Fire of 1748 and become known for its trade in rum, when it was frequented by 'nothing but aquatic captains'. The Jamaica Wine House was established in 1869, and there it stands, up an old alleyway, beckoning with tamer substances a suited clientele who make their money in banking highrises rather than on the high seas.

CHAMPAGNE AT THE TOP

4 Vertigo42

MODERN ART ETC.

5 Whitechapel Art Gallery

80–82 Whitechapel High Street

With its commitment to show fine works by known and new international and British artists, the Whitechapel Art Gallery is one of London's premier art galleries, housed in a soaring Arts and Crafts building, designed by Charles Harrison Townsend, off the beaten path in a gritty area of London near the southern end of Brick Lane. Established in 1901 to 'bring great art to the people of the East End of London', the Whitechapel names Picasso, Mark Rothko and Jackson Pollock among its early shows. More recently international contemporary artists Nan Goldin, Mark Wallinger and Carl Andre have held exhibitions in the space.

FROM VEGETABLES TO VINTAGE

6 Spitalfields Market

Commercial Street
• The Square Pie Company

One of London's liveliest and most varied markets, old Spitalfields contains everything from antiques to jewelry and textiles created by design-school graduates. A market was first held in the 13th century in the fields near St Mary Spital hospital and fruit and vegetables continued to be sold in the same area until 1991, when the market was relocated. Although the western section has been demolished, much of the Victorian structure has been preserved as an indoor space for stall-holders selling organic produce, ethnic foods and fresh bread, as well as crafts, second-hand clothes and wooden toys. The best day to catch the full range of goods is on Sunday, and every day except Saturday, you can supplement your shopping energy with a stop at the Square Pie Company, a tidy, red-tiled stand serving handmade authentic British pies in their trademark square design.

PERIOD DRAMA

7 Dennis Severs's House

18 Folgate Street

California artist Dennis Severs fell in love with Spitalfields and its history, but his stunning re-creation of early-18th-century life in a London townhouse is an experience unlike any historic or museum study. Severs lived in the house, which he saved from dereliction, with all the trappings of the period, and until his death in 1999 personally escorted guests and visitors around the house in a complete sensory experience. Using everything from period furnishings and art, clothes, utensils and food, he aimed to 'bombard your senses'. 'I will get the 20th century out of your eyes, ears and everything,' he said. The house remains open to occasional tours, and each one is like a journey into an Old Master painting. Meandering silently through the candlelit rooms during evening tours, you are transported far beyond historical reconstruction.

8   Christ Church, Spitalfields

Commercial Street

Christ Church is considered one of the best churches designed by Nicholas Hawksmoor, the eccentric successor to Christopher Wren. Designed in 1714 directly opposite Spitalfields market, it has an outsized tower and sober spire that are classic idiosyncratic Hawksmoor features in what is often called the English Baroque. The church is largely intact, despite having been struck by lightning in 1841 and subsequently 'repaired'. With its four great Tuscan-style columns, the portico makes a grand entrance, while the interior follows a simple, graceful design.

MODERN GEMS

9   Ben Day

18 Hanbury Street

After 16 years as a jeweler in London and Los Angeles, Ben Day has settled in his native city, founding his atelier and shop space in the old Huguenot quarter of London. Noted as a true artisan with his pieces making frequent appearances in the fashion press, Day works with coloured gems, pearls and precious metals to produce jewelry of chunky simplicity, and was recently invited to join Selfridge's (see p. 166) new men's brand. His shop is also a glittering little gem.

WHERE CURRY MEETS CUTTING EDGE

10   Brick Lane

- Tatty Devine, no. 236
- Unto This Last, no. 230
- Overdose on Design, no. 182
- @ Work, no. 156
- Vibe Bar, nos 91–95
- Boiler House, opposite Truman Brewery
- Brick Lane Beigel Bake, no. 159
- Le Taj, nos 96, 134

A street long associated with its Asian inhabitants, where the concentration of Indian and ethnic restaurants and the lively Sunday market that fills the lane with stalls and bargain-hunters, Brick Lane has most recently become a centre of cutting-edge art and design. Starting from north (above Bethnal Green Road) is Tatty Devine, selling avant-garde jewelry, T-shirts and art from its brick-red shopfront. A few doors down (open on Sundays only), Paris-born Olivier Geoffroy has set up his furniture shop, Unto This Last, in a former pub to sell his beautifully formed birch-ply tables, chairs, bookshelves and room accessories.

Crossing Bethnal Green Road you enter the area of Brick Lane proper, where the first indication of the design takeover is Overdose on Design. Stop by @Work for innovative and uninhibited jewelry designs. In front of the Truman Brewery office complex is Vibe Bar, whose dance-tinged music remains a solid favourite. Across the lane and slightly south an unmarked door leads to the vast club space that is the Boiler House, a converted warehouse that hosts a variety of club nights, exhibitions and a relaxed café. After clubbing, head for the 24-hour Brick Lane Beigel Bake, but be prepared to stand in a queue and shout your order. Past the Truman Brewery (see next entry) and the art space opposite, the realm of Indian and Bangladeshi restaurants begins. The trend for clean, spare design, with modernized ethnic cuisine is heralded by Le Taj (at 96 and 134), featuring an excellent, innovative menu of Indian and Bangladeshi cuisine.

ARTISTIC EXPRESSIONS

11   Truman Brewery

91–95 Brick Lane
- Café 1001, 1 Dray Walk
- Junky, 12 Dray Walk

The Truman Brewery complex is now host to exhibitions of up-and-coming young artists, and is identifiable by the bridge over Brick Lane (at about its midpoint). A small walkway that is today a shoplined pedestrian area, Dray Walk is heralded by the bright-orange Café 1001, a good place to stop for a toasted focaccia sandwich, a fruit smoothie or coffee. Further down are exhibition spaces, and shops selling funky T-shirts and trainers. Junky offers 'recycled' clothes: new fashion-designer wear that has been bought as overstock and completely reinvented – a man's suit jacket becomes a women's halter, a pinstriped suit becomes a pair of 'magic trousers' and lovely 'patchwork' skirts.

SIMPLE AND RELIABLE

12   Labour and Wait

10 Cheshire Street

Cheshire Street has become a magnet of quaint speciality shops. Rachel Wythe-Moran and Simon Watkins were already working together when they discovered a shared 'passion for good, functional, honest products'. In their premises near the market district of Brick Lane they stock an array of such items of 'classic, timeless' quality. There is a certain Zen-like utilitarian beauty about most of the things they sell, from wooden pencil boxes and rope products to enamelware and watering cans.

Some of his pieces are available in Selfridge's (p. 166), but this is the only retail source for the complete Pauric Sweeney. An Irish designer with a taste for collage, he first found success as a jewelry designer but soon became known for his women's fashion collection, first shown at the Louvre in 2000. He's been a Shoreditch resident since 1996, and when he opened his shop in 1999 his collections were an immediate hit. Sweeney sells his own-design jewelry, as well as bags, belts and ready-to-wear in a style he describes as gothic. His customized Adidas track suits caught the attention of Madonna, who bought the entire collection. He raised eyebrows in 2004 with a catwalk show featuring tabloid models dressed only in accessories.

An area as steeped in creativity as Shoreditch would not be complete without a funky bookshop devoted to the subject. Whimsical, authoritative and up-to-date publications keep track of the latest trends in the ever-changing world of contemporary art.

If you cannot find what you like among their over 500 brands in stock, including its own unique label, then you can order it from them (or their website). Once you're in the door, there'll be something you'll just have to try.

TRUE ECCENTRIC

16 The Foundry

84–86 Great Eastern Street

This unlikely bar, teetering on the corner of a busy intersection, stubbornly refuses to give in to the wave of gentrification sweeping the area. The Foundry is a resolutely unfinished space where all is high bohemia. Disused televisions and computer monitors suspended from the ceiling or mounted on display; an arrangement of toy dolls hanging near the entrance, silver-wrapped ceiling services, a small van that dispenses hot coffee in the mornings; and everywhere chipped plaster and paint and worn-out furniture – there is artistic spirit here, supported by its lively and often bizarre programme of performances and exhibitions.

ALL NIGHTER

17 Cargo

158

AN EMPIRE OF SALVAGE

18 LASSCO St Michaels

Mark Street (off Paul Street)

The name is an acronym for the London Architectural Salvage and Supply Co. Ltd, and since 1979 it has been a unique source of architectural and ornamental antiques. In their Victorian church premises garden cherubs, church pews, stone gargoyles from building façades, stained glass windows and entire carved doorways can be found among the items from Buckingham Palace, the Tower of London, the Palace of Westminster and the Royal Opera House.

ARTISTIC DEN

19 Dragon Bar

156

GLAMOUR ROCKS

20 Lara Bohinc 107

170

21 Eyre Brothers
70 Leonard Street

David Eyre and his brother Robert are the gastro-publicans par excellence. David Eyre has taken his Mediterranean-inspired dishes into a new realm, here focusing largely on Iberian ingredients and flavours, with a dash of Mozambique, where the Eyres grew up. Try razor clams and jamón Ibérico for starters and octopus with smoked paprika or hare casserole for mains.

LATE-NIGHT DINING STYLE
22 Home
100–106 Leonard Street

What began as a groovy downstairs DJ bar with one room serving Mediterranean fare, has burgeoned into a fully fledged, glass-fronted hip bar and restaurant. A good first stop before hitting the bars of Hoxton Square (p. 159) and environs or a resuscitating last call (it is open until 1 am).

REBIRTH OF COOL
23 Hoxton Square

159

NEW KIDS ON THE BLOCK
24 Hoxton Apprentice
16 Hoxton Square

Before there was Jamie Oliver, there was Prue Leith, famed British chef and restaurateur, who decided to take some disadvantaged young people and give them a chance to learn the restaurant trade. The Hoxton Apprentice shows a serious commitment to making good, innovative cuisine and serving it in a place that feels sophisticated without any pretense. The menu on any given day is limited, allowing staff to focus on quality. A genuine success story for everyone, especially diners.

BRIT-ART EPICENTRE
25 White Cube
48 Hoxton Square

White Cube has become avant-garde art patron Jay Jopling's headquarters, as well as offering 2000 square feet of open, toplit display space under 15-foot ceilings. With a list of artists that includes Damien Hirst, Tracey Emin, Nan Goldin and Lucian Freud, the gallery is a perfect insight into current – if not future – taste in British art.

GRITTY AND HIP
26 Kingsland Road
- Viet Hoa, nos 70–72
- dreambagsjaguarshoes, nos 34–36

Kingsland Road is the place to experience an edgier emerging scene. dreambagsjaguarshoes, whose vestigial sign as a former import shop belies the hipness created by co-owners Nick and Teresa Letchford. North of the bridge, in little Vietnam, lies Viet Hoa, which many people consider to be the best Vietnamese restaurant in London.

ENGLISH INTERIORS
27 Geffrye Museum
Kingsland Road

Interior design and history buffs will not be disappointed in Britain's only museum dedicated to English domestic furniture and decoration, housed in 18th-century almshouses, with a striking 1998 addition by Branson Coates. A chronological sequence of re-created period rooms, begins with a 17th-century oak-panelled vignette, through the refined Georgian period, up to mid-century modern and contemporary interiors.

OVER THE TOP EMBELLISHMENTS
28 Les Trois Garçons
1 Club Row

Three former antiques dealers have taken a spot of the dark and weary Bethnal Green Road and shined it up like a new and brightly coloured jewel. The interiors are a riot of decorative motifs all mixed and matched: a stuffed tiger and alligator, opulent chandeliers, bits of costume jewelry. However, the menu reflects a lot more focus: traditional French-inspired dishes from foie gras and duck breast to tiger prawns.

FLOWER-STREWN STREET
29 Columbia Road

The Columbia Road Flower Market used to be an East London tradition, but now attracts throngs of people who rise early on a Sunday to beat the crowds when the market opens at 8 am. Boasting 'the finest selection of flowers and cut plants in the country', the nursery and 'pitch' owners along the road are constantly bringing in more and increasingly exotic stock, making this one of the most picturesque open markets in Europe.

South Bank
Southwark
Bermondsey

HOLBORN

CITY

TOWER HILL ⊖

The Tower
of London

River Thames

London Bridge

Blackfriars Bridge

Millennium
Foot
Bridge   **6**

Oxo
Tower
Wharf

2

Royal
National
Theatre

SOUTH BANK

5
Tate
Modern

Shakespeare's
Globe   **7**

Southwark Br.

Tooley Street

Tower Bridge

River Thames   Waterloo Bridge

8 Holland St.

12

13
Southwark
Cathedral

City Hall

Stamford Street

SOUTHWARK

LONDON
BRIDGE

15

Desi
Muse

9

Royal
Festival
Hall

Jubilee
Gardens

SOUTHWARK

Southwark Street

Southwark Street

St Thomas Street

Druid St

20

London
Eye

1

WATERLOO

10
The Cut

3

Blackfriars Road

Union Street

Union Street

14

Newcomen St

Bermondsey Street

Tooley Street

Druid Street

York Road

County Hall

11
Webber Street

Southwark Bridge Road

Snowsfields

17

16

18

Jama

Westminster Bridge

Webber Street

BOROUGH ⊖

Borough High Street

Marshalsea Rd

Long Lane

Lambeth Palace Road

Baylis Road

BOROUGH

Borough Road

Great Dover Street

Westminster Bridge Road

LAMBETH
NORTH ⊖

St George's
Circus

Bermondsey
Square

19

Abbey Street

Tower Bridge Road

Houses of
Parliament

Lambeth Road

St George's Road

London Road

Harper Road

BERMONDS

Lambeth
Palace
Gardens

Imperial
War
Museum

Newington Causeway

Lambeth Road

Elephant
&
Castle

Lambeth
Palace

New Kent Road

Lambeth
Bridge

⊖ ELEPHANT
& CASTLE

KENNINGTON

Approximate scale

1 kilometre

1/2 mile

A string of new developments, which have stop-started since the 1980s and finally culminated in the opening of Tate Modern in 2000, have finally galvanized the South Bank into an area greater than the sum of its parts. Until such large-scale and high-profile cultural projects as the Tate (p. 101) and Globe Theatre (p. 102) gave locals and visitors a reason to head south in significant numbers, efforts to rehabilitate the riverine environments, such as the South Bank Centre, Butlers Wharf and the Design Museum, had been isolated and never really gained a critical mass. But what were once noble if disparate ventures are celebrated today as a 'string of pearls'. The London Eye, a terrific testimony to British design and engineering, and the ovoid Greater London Authority building designed by Norman Foster are fitting symbols of the South Bank's arrival. The Thames River Walk on the south provides spectacular views to the regal north shore as well as allowing a glimpse into a genuinely different side of London on the south.

Large-scale new building developments and local regeneration have in turn gradually been revivifying areas that had fallen into decay. The area immediately behind the Tate, usually referred to as Borough, is seeing an explosion of loft developments and design studios. Local markets, such as Borough (for fruit, vegetables and speciality food items) and Bermondsey (antiques), which have been operating for decades, if not centuries, are now attracting a more affluent clientele and international visitors. The legendary Old Vic theatre (p. 105) received a boost when it was taken over by a charitable trust in 2000 and then raised its profile even higher when actor Kevin Spacey took over as director in 2004. The cooperative building Oxo Tower symbolizes local community spirit while promoting design talent and innovative crafts. And the completion of the Millennium Bridge has provided further stimulus: lunching City bankers and visitors to St Paul's can stroll effortlessly across the Thames to another world.

Compared with other parts of London, there are still relatively few places for stylish eating and drinking, but this is beginning to change. Arty cafés (such as Delfina, p. 106), galleries, even gastro-pubs are beginning to pop up – and most appear to have staying-power (though there is as yet no hotel that caters to the chic or cultured). As you wander down the Thames River Walk, you may be tempted to eat at one of the museum restaurants – some of which are very good indeed, like the People's Palace in the South Bank Centre (p. 102) – but it's often worth the detour to find the locales that cater to the savvy residents rather than to the tourists.

1 London Eye

Jubilee Gardens

It was a less-publicized and non-government-funded millennium project, but it must be the most enduringly successful in terms of public enjoyment. Standing in front of the new Jubilee Gardens between the Royal Festival Hall and the County Hall and conceived by architects David Marks and Julia Barfield, the graceful giant of a ferris wheel is a true marriage of design and engineering. Each glass-enclosed pod carries around 20 people and allows for uninterrupted views from its top height at 135 metres (450 feet) above the Thames. It takes 30 minutes for a full rotation of the 32 capsules, which means that the thrill of the ride is all in the eye.

RIVERSIDE VIEWS

2 Oxo Tower

Bargehouse Street

Before 1996, the places where you could have a good meal and enjoy a panoramic view of the Thames were virtually nonexistent. The Oxo Tower redevelopment, the felicitous victory of a neighbourhood coalition over hungry developers, changed all that when its top-floor restaurant and brasserie (designed by Lifshutz Davidson) opened (in association with posh department store Harvey Nichols) in the old tower building formerly belonging to the makers of bouillon cubes. The building now combines low-rent housing with retail design studios for 33 designers and makers on the first and second floors. The restaurant and brasserie-bar have breathtaking views and an open-air terrace. Prices tend to relate to the view rather than the food, so, given the choice, the brasserie's changing global menu is a better bet.

NEW, COOL AND SLAVIC

3 Baltic

74 Blackfriars Road

Sleek, stylish, modern and eastern European, Baltic has
turned a contemporary eye to Slavic cuisine with a cool,
tasteful design more often seen in the West End than
south of the river. The tall, open interior was once a
workshop for coach building, but has been stunningly
remodelled. The inventive menu ranges from seasoned
crayfish in vodka butter to venison with cherries, with
dashes of caviar, beetroot and blinis in between. Service is
as smooth as the interior decoration and low-amplitude
jazz serenades the clientele venturing down from the
financial district across the river. A slick bar serves a host
of Polish vodkas and a spectrum of interesting, vodka-
based cocktails.

THE POWER OF ART

4 Tate Modern

Bankside

The former Bankside Power Station designed by Giles
Gilbert Scott was opened in 1963 but by the 1990s
was disused and regarded by many as an eyesore. Through
the vision of Tate director Nicholas Serota and Swiss
architects Herzog & de Meuron the massive building was
transformed to house the collections that make up the
Tate Modern, international art from 1900 to the present,
including important works by Dalí, Picasso and Matisse,
as well as contemporary artists. The former Turbine Hall,
which runs the whole length of the vast building, makes
a grand gallery entrance not unlike a cathedral space. In
addition to the galleries, which feature permanent and
temporary exhibitions, there are a café and art bookshop
– the largest in Europe – on the ground floor. The top-
floor restaurant, serving modern British cuisine, has
glorious views over the Thames.

5 Tate to Tate Boat Service
quai at Tate Britain or Tate Modern

The Tate to Tate boat service launched by Thames Clippers in May 2003 follows an artistic river route from the Tate Modern (see p. 101) to the original Tate Britain museum. The boat, which also makes a stop at the London Eye (p. 100), is a rather eye-catching vessel whose colourful spotty design was specially commissioned from British artist Damien Hirst. As well as transporting you from one cultural spot to the next, the boat trip allows for a fantastic cruising view of waterfront landmarks such as the Houses of Parliament, the South Bank Centre and Somerset House.

ENGINEERING WONDER
6 Millennium Bridge
Bankside

A competition to build a pedestrian bridge spanning the Thames, the first in central London in over a century, to link the Tate Modern with St Paul's Cathedral has resulted in what must be the most dramatic and beautiful of London's bridges. Designed by Norman Foster in close collaboration with sculptor Anthony Caro and world-renowned engineering firm Arup, it is an artistic and engineering masterwork. The 325-metre-long (1,070-foot) 'blade-like' shallow bridge is an entirely new concept in suspension bridges. Walking across on a moonlit night after an evening at the Globe or dinner at Tate Modern, headed for the lighted, magisterial form of St Paul's, is truly an exhilarating London experience. A stroll during the day is pretty uplifting too.

HAPPY RECREATION
7 Shakespeare's Globe
21 new Globe Walk, Bankside

American actor Sam Wanamaker's dream to re-create Shakespeare's Globe Theatre was realized in 1997. With open-air wood stage and galleries, thatched roof and uncovered 'yard' – the standing area where the 'groundlings' who paid a penny for their entry would have stood while drinking beer, munching peanuts and oranges and regularly heckling the actors on stage – the Globe is a faithful reconstruction of the original Elizabethan theatre. Visitors today can stand in the yard for around five pounds. Performances, many of which are true to their Elizabethan originals and highly regarded by theatre critics and public, take place in all weathers, despite the lack of a roof.

RARE AND OUT-OF-PRINT
8 Marcus Campbell Art Books
43 Holland Street

After your visit to the Tate Modern you might want to wander over to Marcus Campbell, conveniently located across the street. Campbell specializes in books on late-20th-century art and artists, with a particular focus on rare and out-of-print artists' books by and about such figures as Sol LeWitt, Ed Ruscha, Marcel Broodthaers, Lawrence Weiner and Gilbert and George. 'Conceptual art when it began', Campbell says, and 'the historical stuff is what interests me'.

MAGNET FOR THE ARTS
9 South Bank Centre
• People's Palace
• Royal Festival Hall
• Hayward Gallery

Although many decry the South Bank Centre's concrete brutalism, built as the centrepiece in 1951 for the forward-looking Festival of Britain, its position today as one of London's most important cultural attractions is undisputed. The flexible exhibition spaces of the Hayward Gallery are dedicated principally to shows of modern and contemporary art. With three auditoriums, temporary exhibition spaces and outdoor performances, the South Bank Centre is a constant hive of activity. On the third level of the Royal Festival Hall is the People's Palace restaurant, serving British modern cuisine. The dramatic and minimal room includes a bar and has stunning views of the river and the city beyond along its 36-metre-long (120-foot) glass front.

FOOD, GLORIOUS FOOD
10 Anchor & Hope
36 The Cut

In the current maelstrom of British gastro-pub dining wars the Anchor & Hope holds its own, offering a carnival of rich, hearty eating. And whether it is grouse or teal, herring or ham that you are hankering, the dishes are well-rounded with appropriate accompaniments: red cabbage, duck fat potato cakes, lentils, prunes, figs, or a bouquet of green salad. The interior is suitably rustic and spare, while the chefs, formerly of St John (p. 144) and the Fox, another gastro-pub success story, have kept up an award-winning menu since opening in 2003. They don't take bookings, so getting there early is the only way to guard against disappointment.

11 Old Vic Theatre

Waterloo Road

One of the oldest theatres in London and the only surviving venue dating from the Regency period (founded 1818), the Old Vic has a worldwide reputation as 'the actors' theatre'. Laurence Olivier, John Gielgud, Alec Guiness, Ralph Richardson, Peter O'Toole, Judi Dench and Maggie Smith have all trod the boards here, but the future was in jeopardy when the theatre came up for sale. Fortunately a charitable trust took over in 2000, and popular interest grew when Kevin Spacey took over as director in 2004. His first production, the dark comedy *Cloaca*, by Dutch writer Maria Goos got mixed reviews, but such 'teething problems' haven't dimmed the bright future predicted for the old favourite under Spacey's guidance.

CITY OF WINE

12 Vinopolis

1 Bank End

'Uncork your mind; indulge your senses' is the motto of this modern temple to the grape along the Millennium Mile on the South Bank of the Thames. A wine museum that features an interactive virtual tour through all the wine-growing regions of the world, it contains enough history and information to make you drunk on facts. Luckily there is also the revered product itself, available at tasting tables along the way and sold in the adjacent wine store. Even if you're just stopping by, there's a vast selection to be had by the glass or bottle in the Wine Wharf bar as well as in the Michelin-rated Cantina Vinopolis.

GOTHIC ORIGINAL

13 Southwark Cathedral

Montague Close

The earliest Gothic church in London was built as St Mary Overie in 1220 and became the parish church of St Saviour, Southwark, in 1539. It suffered fires and periods of neglect until it was bought from James I in 1614 by the parishioners, who have looked after it ever since. Happily, it was not damaged during the Civil War, and the current tower with four pinnacles was finished in 1689. Among the many wonderful tributes, monuments and gifts inside is a 13th-century carved oak effigy of a knight and another of John Gower, who was a friend to Chaucer and himself a poet (Chaucer's pilgrims in the *Canterbury Tales* set off from a spot near here). Inside the south-west entrance the Gothic arcading is still visible, which was rebuilt after a fire

in 1206. At one end of the north aisle are 12 ceiling bosses taken from the 15th-century wooden roof that collapsed in 1830. They depict vices such as malice, gluttony and falsehood, as well as heraldic sunflowers and roses. Piers, chancel and other elements from the 13th century survived, along with many wonderful later pieces, such as the carved monument to Alderman Humble and his wives, dressed in their 17th-century best. The monument to Shakespeare is 20th century, but there is a funeral paving stone belonging to the Bard's brother Edmund (d. 1607).

HISTORIC PLEASURE

14 The George Inn

77 Borough High Street

On a cobbled courtyard off Borough High Street is London's only surviving galleried coaching inn, a rare example of a medieval pub in the city. Destroyed by fire and rebuilt in 1676, it has escaped demolition many times and is now protected by the National Trust. Its distinctive whitewashed but yellowed walls, oak beams, wood panelling and lattice windows evoke another era beyond the modern-day traffic outside. Dickens is said to have been a regular in one of the series of room-sized bars that make up the ground floor. The former bedchambers upstairs have long since been converted to dining and public rooms but have lost none of their gloriously aged character in the transition.

CONRAN'S EMPIRE

15 The Gastrodome

Shad Thames

Terence Conran has come a long way since setting up his furniture-making business in 1952. First came Habitat and the eponymous design shops, then he turned his hand to food, and the London dining experience has not been the same since. His row of restaurants and gourmet food shops along the south bank of the Thames helped catalyze the revitalization of the area, along with the establishment of the Design Museum (p. 107) and its Blue Print Café. Within a single enclave are the unabashedly British Butlers Wharf Chop House, the refined, French-influenced, seafood-oriented Pont de la Tour and the relaxed, Italophile Cantina del Ponte. Conran has ten other restaurants around London in established areas, but it is the Gastrodome's location amid former derelict riverside warehouses (now mainly lofts), with gorgeous views towards the Tower of London and the City, that makes it a world of its own.

THE ARTFUL LUNCHER

16 Delfina

50 Bermondsey Street

Located on a characterful street, Delfina started out as a warehouse that had been converted into studio space for artists by patron Delfina Entrecanales. The café for resident artists soon became a popular lunchtime spot, and today it helps to support the studio programme and provides public exhibition space. Its white-walled surroundings are a fitting backdrop to the changing collection of artworks, and even the labels on the wine bottles are works of art, produced by Turner Prize–nominee Tacita Dean. Maria Eilia is the artist in the kitchen, producing modern Mediterranean dishes such as seared tuna and chorizo risotto, in a menu that changes fortnightly.

PATTERN PRODIGIES

17 Eley Kishimoto

168

TEXTILES AND ARCHITECTURE

18 Fashion and Textile Museum

83 Bermondsey Street

Extravagant fashion designer Zandra Rhodes and Mexican architect Ricardo Legorreta have conspired to shake up the brick lanes of Bermondsey with a new museum devoted to fashion. Legorreta's characteristic swathes of colour – bright orange and pink – do for building what Rhodes has done for fashion for decades. According to Rhodes, the museum is 'the first of its kind, to showcase the work of local and international fashion and textile designers'. It will also serve students in the industry by offering fellowships. This latest grand architectural project to grace the South Bank has an interior as striking as the exterior, with sculptural spaces in monochrome white, pink and blue.

19 Bermondsey Market

Bermondsey Square

This pre-dawn, Friday-only market held in a quiet square has legendary status among Londoners. The enchantment has to do with its early opening hours, a consequence, it is generally believed, of the fact that objects sold before sunrise are not subject to laws regarding handling of stolen goods. The reality is that this is London's most vibrant antiques market, a feeding ground mostly for dealers and knowledgable early risers – prices do so after 9 am. Jewelry and silver are the mainstays of the market, but paintings, china, rugs and a host of bric-à-brac are all to be had for the right, often negotiable, sum.

20 Design Museum

28 Shad Thames

Billed as 'the world's first museum dedicated to the study of contemporary design', the Design Museum's collection and exhibitions keep the world of product design open and accessible to the general public. Today, under the dynamic directorship of Alice Rawsthorn, the Design Museum presents a broad spectrum of exhibitions, covering all facets of design, from graphics to product design. Testament to her vision have been recent exhibitions on France's darlings of furniture design, the Bourellec brothers, and 'When Isabella met Philip', on the hats Philip Treacy (p. 167) designed for fashion patron Isabella Blow. In addition to the exhibition spaces are a bookshop selling a range of desirable design objects and the Blue Print Café, which serves modern interpretations of 'comfort food' against stupendous views over the city.

Style Traveller

sleep

London's best hotels are famed for their discreet service and attention to detail. Although it was not until relatively recently that London responded to the global trend for stylish, more individualistic accommodation, there is now an incomparable array of establishments, ranging from the ultramodern to the ingeniously or ironically traditional. Here is a selection of the best hard-to-find hideaways, small (from three-room) mid-modern meccas, accessibly grand bolt-holes and over-the-top tributes to minimalism, their distinct character reflecting the charisma and vision of their founders.

72 **The Zetter**

5 86-88 Clerkenwell Road
Rooms from £150

Period architecture with contemporary design flair; all mod cons and an environmental conscience, hip location and reasonable rates: the Zetter is a host of lively contrasts. Michael Benyan and Mark Sainsbury, the duo behind the Zetter, have had a string of restaurant successes behind them: The Quality Chop House (p. 76) and, with Sam and Sam Clark, Moro (p. 77), among them. With the Zetter they combined a stylish bar and restaurant on the ground floor with rooms located around an atrium above, in their words, 'a modern-day urban inn', where people could 'meet, eat or sleep'. Beyond that they managed successfully to integrate the historic architecture of a Victorian warehouse building with minimal but striking elements of new design. With 59 rooms on five floors, the Zetter maintains a high level of quality and comfort on a relatively small scale. At the top of the building, seven rooftop studios have been added on with floor-to-ceiling windows and French doors leading to rooftop patio spaces.

Design touches such as art pieces, textiles and wall panels add glamour to the large-proportioned spaces. While home comforts include hot water bottles and books for borrowing. The Zetter also has eco cred. Sustainable materials were used in the design: the bathroom basins are made from recycled plastic; the atrium provides natural ventilation; and the hotel has its own well, which in addition to providing water for air conditioning, is also the source for the still and sparkling drinking water on offer. Situated near the confluence of the financial centre of the City, the cultural hub of Bloomsbury and the bohemian base of Clerkenwell, the Zetter provides guests with a starting point for a range of London experiences. Crafts by local makers are available at the Penneybank studios just behind the hotel in St John's Square; new British design objects can be sampled at Her House (p. 76) around the corner and some of the city's best new British cuisine is to be had at St John, just a few minutes' walk away (p. 144).

42 **Hazlitt's**

39 6 Frith Street

Rooms from £240

'In art, in taste, in life, in speech, you decide from feeling, and not from reason.'
So wrote the great essayist, critic and Napoleon biographer William Hazlitt in 1822.
With such inspiration in mind, Douglas Bain and Peter McKay set out to create
a home away from home in a set of three of Soho's most characterful houses, built
in 1718 and where Hazlitt died, purportedly of drinking too much tea, on 18
September 1830 in what was then a boarding house. Set on a bustling street and
surrounded by creative agencies, restaurants and bars, Hazlitt's is a world away
from 21st-century global London, a discreet and intimate hideaway from the
modern world. Guests who desire a long-lost quintessentially English experience
will experience the words that Hazlitt requested for his gravestone, GRATEFUL
AND CONTENTED.

But don't let the 23 rooms' carved mahogany four-poster beds, Victorian claw-
foot tubs (some original to the house), the rich, bold colours of the walls and fabrics
(the hotel was completely remodelled in 2001), the small sitting rooms and
wonky floors and the absence of elevators fool you, this is the haunt of the
media, antiques collectors and dignitaries who sense that there is something very
special about Hazlitt's and far removed from corporate modern. The staff might
be stylish and amenities contemporary, but the contrast wouldn't have bothered
Hazlitt, who observed, 'We are not hypocrites in our sleep.'

28 | **Cadogan London**
20 | 75 Sloane Street
Rooms from £290

Completed in 1888, the Cadogan Hotel is now forever associated with its two most prominent patrons: Lillie Langtry and Oscar Wilde. Langtry, mistress of Edward VII, lived at 21 Pont Street, which became amalgamated with the hotel. Wilde, who was an admirer of the famous actress, and stayed at the Cadogan partly in order to be close to her, was arrested here on charges of having committed offences against young men, and escorted from room 118, now the Oscar Wilde Room. The Edwardian hotel had become a bit rough around the edges when Grace Leo-Andrieu, of GLA Hotels, took over management and oversaw the redecoration of the first two floors at the end of 2003. Now the ground floor public rooms are shined up in period splendour, with generous swag draperies, polished woodwork and grand proportions, even the conference room has a touch of period elegance about it.

The crowning achievements, however, are the rooms named for the Cadogan's most famous residents. The Lillie Langtry is all fluff and flowers, a boudoir decked in rose wallpaper, pink lace, satin and feather boas. Added to the feminine finery is the prime position of the room overlooking Sloane Square. The Oscar Wilde is somewhat more masculine but no less indulgent, with blue-grey velvet and silvery tafetta. A corner room, it features a bay of three windows that emphasize the tall ceiling height. Other rooms are more restrained but carry the theme of fine furnishing and luxurious fabrics throughout. Rooms on the upper floors have yet to be refurbished by Leo-Andrieu but retain an old-fashioned charm that has been brightened with modern touches. All residents are allowed access to the lovely Cadogan Gardens and tennis courts across from the hotel, which are only open to residents. Shopping and dining on Pont Street, Sloane Square and most of Knightsbridge is walkable. Top off your visit with a meal at Tom Aikens (p. 145) for luxury of a more contemporary kind.

It is hard to say what delights most about this hidden gem. There is the tricky access off a tree-shaded, pedestrianized alley near bustling Smithfield Market, before one steps across the threshold of what seems like someone's private house. Once inside, there are the 33 eccentrically appointed bedrooms, each named after a local character who once lived near by, thus imbuing the four Georgian houses that make up this quintessentially London townhouse hotel not only with period charm, but with real personality. Smithfield is an area that was once known for lawlessness – Charles Dickens's Fagin is said to have haunted its streets – being outside the City's jurisdiction. Areas such as these were known as 'rookeries' and though Smithfield is now full of smartly dressed City workers, clubbers and restaurant patrons, the edgy atmosphere has not completely disappeared, all of which makes for a rather irresistible mix of 'olde-worlde' intrigue and modern sophistication.

As you might expect, The Rookery is a labour of love, created by Douglas Bain and Peter McKay, who have artfully combined the old and new in a romantic, quirky but detail-conscious atmosphere. All of the modern amenities are on tap, while a careful refurbishment and restoration of the original furnishings and fittings that draws on Bain's and McKay's extensive antiques knowledge – wardrobes, secretaires, great carved four-poster beds or Gothic-style bedsteads, period oak panelling, even the Victorian commodes – have taken place with the idea that 'history is always more appealing when it has been cleaned up a bit'. Specialist craftsmen were hired to restore the period plumbing fixtures and adapt them to modern pipework.

The hotel's *pièce de résistance* is the incomparable 'Rook's Nest', a top-level suite with the same carefully honed period feel, enhanced by a restored Edwardian bathing machine, but with a hidden extra: the ceiling opens to reveal a rooftop sitting room accessed by a small stair where guests can enjoy their own private panorama of London. Downstairs, life is less heady, but no less luxurious.

60 The Sanderson

13 50 Berners Street
Rooms from £260

Nouvelle baroque, a study in white, a whimsical if not surreal medley in quirky furniture pieces housed in a protected 1960s office building – the ironic design element of Ian Schrager's seventh hotel masterpiece (and collaboration with Philippe Starck) is in its most exalted form just north of Soho. Indeed, according to Schrager, his 'urban spa' is one of his most daring and at times surprising enterprises, located in an unlikely edifice (the word 'Sanderson' is the only giveaway – even New York art director Fabien Baron couldn't do away with this vestige of preservation requirements) in an unlikely street populated by contract furniture sellers and accountants. Perhaps this is what elevates the Sanderson experience beyond the obvious and well-located appeal of other Schrager confections.

Tucked away beyond the lobby's 1970 Dalí 'Bocca' sofa, Louis XV–style furniture and Venetian mirrors are the Long Bar, a global destination bar complete with a 25-metre (80-foot) onyx bar and international food; Spoon+, the first import from celebrated Parisian superchef Alain Ducasse; and Agua, a diaphanous two-storey, 1000-square-metre (10,000-square-foot) spa sanctuary catering to the world-weary. Other delights and surprises lie behind the irreverent décor: an unexpected Eastern-inspired courtyard (also serving the restaurant) and a bamboo roof garden with views over the capital.

Guest rooms are perhaps variations on a theme of white, but that's no matter when the sheets have a 450-thread count; the mock sleigh beds are silver-leaved and bathroom areas obscured behind opaque silk drapes. Indeed, Starck's room designs are more a play of transparency and opacity (and vanity?) than anything else.

28 **Knightsbridge Hotel**

28 10 Beaufort Gardens
Rooms from £210

'Affordable chic in the heart of Knightsbridge' is how hoteliers and interior designers Tim and Kit Kemp describe their latest venture in London, a new take on a 'traditional English bed and breakfast'. Kit Kemp is no amateur designer, having imbued the Covent Garden, the Charlotte Street and the Pelham with her particularly tasteful and eclectic blend of modern and traditional English style. The Knightsbridge she describes as 'fresh, modern English', which is discerned through the specially commissioned fabrics and artwork set off by comfortably traditional sofas, chairs and tables.

There are 44 rooms, and all have been individually designed by Kit Kemp, so they are rich in colour, pattern and texture. There is the 'fuschia room', a room draped in pale greens and deep purples, as well as some with more neutral tones but still bearing light floral touches. Kit Kemp's trademark retro-design Roberts radios are in every room. Her quirky dress mannequins, which she upholsters in varying fabrics, appear in large and small versions, adding to the overall character and charm.

Although there is no restaurant on-site, there is 24-hour room service with a gourmet menu. Continental breakfast is usually taken by room service, though guests can choose to eat in the jungle-themed drawing room or the library, both of which feature outstanding works of British art commissioned for the hotel.

N°11

ENGLISH UNDESIGN
28 Eleven Cadogan Gardens
25 11 Cadogan Gardens
Rooms from £240

A stone's throw from Sloane Square, marked only by a single sign 'No. 11', Eleven Cadogan Gardens is a genuine late-Victorian testament to what makes the English hotel unique: understatement, discretion, an apparently undesigned interior that works wonderfully, and a just a hint of the aristocratic. It's not hard to understand why it is reportedly design guru Philippe Starck's favourite London hotel. Though one must resist the urge to use superlatives (particularly inappropriate in this context), there is an authenticity, warmth and ease that makes a stay at Eleven Cadogan Gardens an experience you would have only here, in the heart of Chelsea, which means that the high volume of loyal repeat guests can make getting a room tricky at times.

Today's establishment began life in the late 19th century, when Lord Chelsea built four mansions on his cricket ground near Buckingham Palace, which soon become London's first private townhouse hotel. Today, there remain 60 rooms (ask for one of the ones at the back, which overlook beautifully manicured gardens), rich wood-panelled walls, oil paintings, an oak staircase and countless antiques, along with two Garden Suites, one that offers a private entrance and the other featuring a large drawing room that overlooks the garden.

There is no reception desk, but a butler greets visitors at the door, signifying the level of service to follow. Guests handsign a well-worn ledger before being escorted to their premises. Tucked discreetly away in the building are modern amenities, such as a gym and beauty treatment room, reluctant concessions, no doubt, to contemporary travellers. To round out the picture, guests are offered afternoon tea in the dining room, along with fresh cakes, sherry and canapes – what else?

West Street

13–15 West Street
Rooms from £150

The small, detail-conscious boutique hotel has just got smaller and even more finely wrought – the micro-hotel has arrived in the heart of London's Covent Garden theatre district. Just off the patchy Shaftesbury Avenue is an unexpected delight, artfully concealed to all but a few lucky member-guests. With only three suites designed by hip London architects Sally Mackereth and James Wells, the hotel focuses on quality of experience, location and vibe rather than quantity of rooms and amenities.

The hotel is the brainchild of Christopher Bodker, Rowley Leigh and Marian Scrutton, whose success with such restaurants as Circus and The Avenue have placed them among London's most discerning epicureans. Housed in a building formerly used by Japanese businessmen for dubious exploits, the restaurant and bar occupy the ground and basement floors and three highly individualized suites on the floors above.

The high-gloss White Room features white Carrara marble flooring, red accents in soft and hard furnishing and Constanza lamps. The Stone Room (more a suite) takes its name from the limestone and earthy elements – deep browns, leather, creams – and boasts a fabulous private terrace large enough (70 square metres [700 square feel]) for a good-sized cocktail party and features a private lift. And the double-height Loft, occupying the entire fourth floor, has dark oak floors, green-slate walls and bathroom and bright-orange Tulip chairs designed by Geoffrey Bernett, one of many flourishes that dot these sophisticated chambers.

With the Blue Room – a high-tech screening room – the downstairs bar and its magical 6-metre (20-foot) kinetic sculpture by Richard Clark and Alex MacGregor and a restaurant serving modern Mediterranean cuisine, there's little doubt that size – exquisitely detailed – is everything.

Caroline Main isn't exactly rushing around trying to fill her 4-room/3-suite hotel located around the corner from what is probably Notting Hill's most fashionable 200-metre stretch. In fact, she has never advertised at all during the three years that she has been operating the Main House hotel. She hasn't needed to. Word of mouth is enough to keep this spacious Victorian house, with unmarked entrance, relatively full for most of the year. But it's hard to keep a secret, especially the one about very reasonably priced, roomy, stylish accommodation in London with personalized service that makes you wonder why you ever settled for less. 'Simple and professional' is Main's mantra and it applies to everything from the furnishings (though you could also add a certain flair for design here) to the taxi service she offers to collect you and your luggage from the airport, for which you pay only the fee to the taxi company.

   She is equally strict about the running of the Main House, whose rooms have been stripped of fussy decoration but retain period details and generous proportions. These are not highly kitted-out boxes but airy spaces with large windows, polished wood floors, a few choice antique furnishings and rugs and lots of fresh white linens. The first and second-floor rooms, true to their Victorian design, are the grandest in terms of space and include separate sitting and bath areas, one suite per floor. The top floor is given over to two rooms and a smaller shower room, usually let as a suite for families or people travelling together. Main herself is often on call, along with manager Beatta, to bring tea, biscuits, wine, give local advice and arrange taxis. Guests are free to entertain their own visitors, and a separate doorbell even allows them to answer the door themselves – just like home. This and the lack of signage means that it feels more like a house, says Main. So there, the secret is out.

eat

In the past, few visitors would have seen London as a culinary destination, but that has changed radically over the last ten years. A variety of ethnic restaurants has also been an aspect of the city's cosmopolitanism, but today offers more choice than ever before – everything from European cuisine at the very highest level to exotic fare updated with Western touches. Where London has seen the most notable – and, for the world gourmand, most intriguing – development is in the celebration of its own culinary traditions. Where once the visitor faced 'pub grub', today there are a profusion of 'gastro-pubs' – bars serving well-prepared dishes using fresh local ingredients – and New British cuisine tailored to today's more international and demanding palettes.

HIGH-STYLE JAPANESE

| 46 | **Umu** |
| 13 | 14–16 Bruton Place |

There seems to be something of an Oriental invasion happening in the London restaurant scene with Roka (see p. 64), Yauatcha (p. 141) and Hakkasan (p. 133) drawing crowds of upscale diners. Now Umu, an ultra-modern, chic, sophisticated temple of cuisine has arrived with an entrance so discreet on Bruton Place that it's in danger of being overlooked. But it isn't just gimmicky restauranteuring that should bring you to Umu. The décor is wonderful and you do have to press your hand to an electronic glass panel so the unmarked wood door slides open to let you in, but these details are supremely matched by the food, which is traditional Kyoto-style and served either in a set menu or a range of *kaiseiki* options, which are small, beautifully crafted portions. The proprietors are keen to stay true to their roots, even importing water from Japan for some of the cooking. Fish is sourced from all over the world, and a sushi bar lets you get a close look at each species. But such artistic and culinary opulence comes at a price, so be prepared for triple digits.

42

Momo

33 25 Heddon Street

Many say it's all about atmosphere at this unexpected shrine to North African food and décor in Mayfair, but Momo is much more than that. Sandwiched between the Regency façades of Regent Street and sartorial Savile Row is another world dedicated to suffusing the senses with exoticism and extravagance – the contrast couldn't be more London. It would all feel rather themed had Momo not been the product of Mourad Mazouz, whose own travels account for many of the objects that provide the backdrop to the elevated Maghreb (Moroccan, Tunisian, Algerian) cuisine. Look out for echouia salad with chickpea croquettes; vegetable soup with saffron and lemon; sweet and spicy pigeon pie with almonds and cumin. For those in search of less full-on immersion, Casablanca can be experienced remotely in the adjacent tea-room. Below is Kemia, a favourite of princes and princesses from near and far and one of London's more desirable nightspots, for members only Thursday to Saturday but open 'by invitation' on other nights.

60

Hakkasan

19 8 Hanway Place

As you make your way from the teeming throngs of Tottenham Court Road and Oxford Street down a rather unsavoury alleyway, nothing can prepare you for this exquisite bar and restaurant, which combines stylish modern-exotic design with a delicate Singaporean-tinged cuisine. Through the doors you step out of a gritty urban backstreet down into a seductively lit, slate-lined stair and into a sensuous aquamarine environment masterfully created by French designer Christian Liaigre. London's fashionable set prefer to queue for the evening scene, but the best time to go is at lunch, when a modern Dim Sum menu, prepared by head chef Tong Chee Hwee (formerly of Summer Pavilion at Singapore's Ritz Carlton), is available against purple-illuminated glass, fretted-wood partitions and dark wood – continents away from London and worlds away from the mass retail frenzy above. You needn't stop at Dim Sum, for a more complete, contemporary Chinese menu for lunch and dinner is available, as are Asian-tinted cocktails conceived by one of London's master mixers.

Claiming to be London's oldest restaurant, Rules has been going continuously since Thomas Rule first opened it in 1798, when it was known for its 'porter, pies and oysters'. Over the centuries, royalty and celebrity have filled its room: it was known as the haunt of Edward VII when Prince of Wales and his mistress, the actress Lillie Langtry, who made such a habit of visiting that a private door was added so they could avoid the prying eyes of the public; Charles Dickens, Graham Greene and H. G. Wells were frequent diners. It is still devoted to distinctly British meat and game – rabbit, deer, grouse and the prized Belted Galloway cattle – which comes directly from the restaurant's own estates in Lartington in England's High Pennines to ensure the highest standards. A recently restored and beautifully atmospheric dining room, preserved by the last of only three owning families over the decades, provides handsomely for the 'rakes, dandies and superior intelligences who comprise its clientele'. Living London culture and history are alive and well in Covent Garden.

Rules

LONDON'S OLDEST RESTAUR

IN THE YEAR NAPOLEON OPENED HIS CAMPAIGN
THOMAS RULE PROMISED HIS DESPAIRING FAMI
SAY GOODBYE TO HIS WAYWARD PAST, SETTLE
OYSTER BAR IN COVENT GARDEN.

RULES SERVES THE TRADITIONAL FOOD OF THI
BEST — IT SPECIALISES IN CLASSIC GAME COO
FORTUNATE IN OWNING AN ESTATE IN THE HIG
"ENGLAND'S LAST WILDERNESS" WHICH, SUP
RESTAURANT AND WHERE IT IS ABLE TO EXER
CONTROLS AND DETERMINE HOW THE GAME IS

THROUGHOUT ITS LONG HISTORY THE TABLES O
CROWDED WITH WRITERS, ARTISTS, LAWYERS,
ACTORS. AS WELL AS BEING FREQUENTED BY GR
TALENTS — CHARLES DICKENS, WILLIAM MAKEPE
GALSWORTHY & H G WELLS, RULES HAS ALSO
BY ROSAMOND LEHMANN, EVELYN WAUGH, GRAH
LE CARRÉ, DICK FRANCIS AND CLAIRE RAYNER

ON THE FIRST FLOOR, BY THE LATTICE WINDOW

42
Adam Street

51 9 Adam Street
Lunch only (for non-members)

Like the most intriguing city addresses, you wouldn't know it was there unless you were looking for it. A plaque announces a private members' club just off the Strand, and the bell suggests the uninvited are not to wander in. Fortunately you don't have to be a member to book a table in the restaurant for lunch, though descending the red-carpeted staircase does deliver the zing of exclusivity. As you step into the subterranean space, you might remember that the dual barrel vaults in which the restaurant and bar are now situated were the foundations of the Adelphi, a development of artists' residences conceived and partly built by master architects Robert and James Adam from 1768 to 1792. Today the space has been modernized, peopled with nearby publishers and features a bar area, with contemporary club chairs and purple velvet stools, while the restaurant is a formal, intimate dining space with classic British dishes (including a revisited macaroni and cheese). A destination after morning gallery visits on Trafalgar Square.

TOWNHOUSE DINING
42
Lindsay House

35 21 Romilly Street

Irish chef Richard Corrigan was awarded a Michelin star for his restaurant, which occupies a 1740 London townhouse in the heart of Soho. Though set in an atmosphere of cheap Italian cafés, pubs and sex shops, the genteel and serene atmosphere of the Lindsay House – which begins as soon as you ring the entrance doorbell – sits in stark contrast to the revelling hoi polloi outside. Two Georgian dining rooms, with preserved period details, high ceilings and minimally added decoration, have an elegantly at-home feel about them, which, despite the high ratio of staff to diners, makes for a warm, intimate and ultimately romantic experience. The menu encompasses a range of lightly fused cuisines from gazpacho of English crayfish to guinea fowl in Madeira, and the wine list is varied and well suited to the exquisitely prepared dishes.

ARCHETYPAL CARVERY
42 **The Grill Room at The Dorchester**
2 53 Park Lane

It's really a shame to visit London without splashing out for a proper carvery in one of the classic grand hotel restaurants. Merely uttering 'The Dorchester' carries a ring of refinement that becomes evident beneath the great Grill Room's gold-leaf-lined coffered ceiling and among the leather armchairs, velvet curtains and Flemish tapestries, all of which are of the 1931 room, when it was known as the Spanish Grill and featured a dedicated sherry bar. Today, the menu celebrates high British cuisine. Head chef Henri Brosi, who came to the Grill Room in 1999 after a period at Claridge's, has embraced the traditional fare with a passion. The grilled dishes include steaks, Scottish lobster, wild salmon and turbot, complemented by such old favourites as roast Aberdeenshire beef with Yorkshire pudding and humble shepherd's pie. Brosi's signature dishes are variations on the traditional – scallops with warm tomato and saffron dressing, or rack of lamb with mustard and herb crust. Having had only seven chefs in the last 70 years, the Grill Room stands as a timeless and unwavering London institution.

OH, VIENNA
42 **The Wolseley**
19 160 Piccadilly

The Wolseley opened in late 2003 to almost instant acclaim and doesn't seem to be losing any popularity. Founders of star-attractors Le Caprice and the Ivy – Jeremy King and Christopher Corbin – took over the former Wolseley car show room to open a grand Old World–style café, with a design by David Collins (see also p. 150). The great ceiling space, a brass-lined bar, reading lamps, treat-filled pastry counter, starched white table cloths and formally trained but friendly service staff make the Wolseley popular with both famous and casual diners. The menu is old-fashioned as well, offering steaks cooked to perfection whichever way you ask for them, and delicately cut chips (if chips can ever be delicate) presented in a jolly paper-wrapped parcel for lunch. Chris Galvin, who once presided over the Michelin-starred Orrery, also oversees omelettes, bratwurst, goulash, Wiener schnitzel, oysters and caviar, with everything conspiring to make customers feel like a Habsburg on holiday. Alas, you have a much better chance of getting in for lunch or the viennosserie-style breakfast than for dinner, which is sometimes booked weeks in advance.

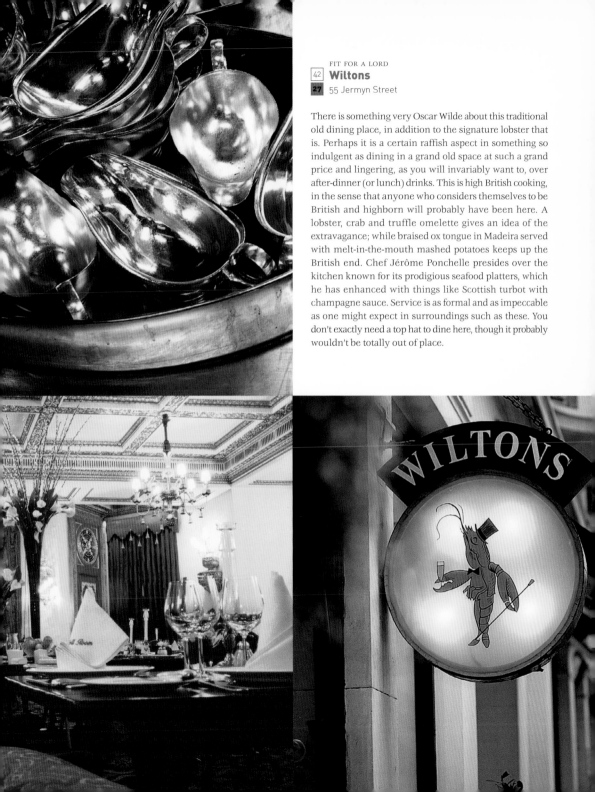

FIT FOR A LORD
Wiltons
`42`
`27` 55 Jermyn Street

There is something very Oscar Wilde about this traditional old dining place, in addition to the signature lobster that is. Perhaps it is a certain raffish aspect in something so indulgent as dining in a grand old space at such a grand price and lingering, as you will invariably want to, over after-dinner (or lunch) drinks. This is high British cooking, in the sense that anyone who considers themselves to be British and highborn will probably have been here. A lobster, crab and truffle omelette gives an idea of the extravagance; while braised ox tongue in Madeira served with melt-in-the-mouth mashed potatoes keeps up the British end. Chef Jérôme Ponchelle presides over the kitchen known for its prodigious seafood platters, which he has enhanced with things like Scottish turbot with champagne sauce. Service is as formal and as impeccable as one might expect in surroundings such as these. You don't exactly need a top hat to dine here, though it probably wouldn't be totally out of place.

NEIGHBOURHOOD JOINT

14 The Cow
17 89 Westbourne Park Road

The Cow, at the periphery of Notting Hill, was a pleasant old-fashioned pub even before it became known for its new menu and speciality, fresh seafood. Owned by Tom Conran, son of restaurateur and design guru Terence, today it is a little pub with a large following and a jolly place to meet for a drink and a plate of oysters, a little slice of Notting Hill life and a favourite of locals despite the occasional visit from a celebrity (Elvis Costello, Uma Thurman, Kylie Minogue and Hugh Grant have stopped by). If a heartier meal is in your sights, you can have a proper repast in the intimate upstairs dining room, which focuses on modern British (you are advised to book ahead). In nice weather, sitting outside on the quiet road in view of the nearby Westbourne (p. 20) you might feel a little spoiled for choice.

THE ORIGINAL GASTRO-PUB

72 The Eagle
11 159 Farringdon Road

Hailed as the first 'gastro-pub' in London, the Eagle began in 1991 what many modernized London pubs are now trying to do with widely varying degrees of success. As owner Michael Belben, who started The Eagle with David Eyre, the Eagle's first chef, says, 'we weren't the first pub to serve good food, but we were probably the first pub to serve extremely good food in casual surroundings'. What they did not want to do was 'exclude traditional drinkers'; nor did they want to include a lot of 'unnecessary trimmings'. So you won't find table linens or complicated selections of courses or even a tab (you pay when you order), but you will find a place that's welcoming for a long drink or a very good dinner, as enjoyed by the nearby journalists and creatives. Wood details and an eclectic mix of well-worn leather sofas, old bar stools and unmatched dining chairs contribute to the casual atmosphere. The daily-changing menu is hearty and leans toward the Mediterranean, though current chef Tom Norrington-Davis says this is because they serve what they think is good, not because they're adhering to style.

All-white tablecloths and high-backed chairs arranged against magnificent soaring white walls in what used to be the 1897 Westminster Library, the Cinnamon Club is the modern, upscale face of Indian food as envisioned by owner Iqbal Wahhab. Original bookshelves, wood screens and parquet flooring have been retained while Indian marble and stone have been incorporated into a clean-lined fusion of colonial convergence. Under chef Vivek Singh, with the help of Michelin-starred French chef Eric Chavot, contemporary Indian cuisine reaches new heights of sophistication and refinement, served to a public ranging from Westminster politicians to jetsetters. Traditional techniques are applied to unconventional ingredients and vice versa, producing acclaimed dishes such as sweet potato cake with crispy okra and spiced yoghurt, duck breast with sesame tamarind sauce and spinach dumplings with chickpea cake, all suggesting that this is a place with staying-power. The downstairs late-night members' bar and lounge serves Indian-tinged cocktails and dance music to ensure your evening ends on a cool note.

42 Sketch

10 9 Conduit Street

Probably the most ambitious and chicest venues to open in the last decade, Sketch – so-called because it is constantly evolving – marks the apotheosis of high design, high style and high gastronomy. A long-term labour of love and passion by Mourad Mazouz (see also p. 133) and set in a Georgian mansion most recently occupied by Christian Dior, Sketch displays a dazzling diversity of design that extends to a parlour, art gallery, two bars, two restaurants and a lecture theatre. No surface has been left unconsidered – from the Swarovski-bejewelled bathrooms to the in-situ artworks; no culinary delight thought too extravagant – Parisian masterchef Pierre Gagnaire has created all the food, from the pastries in the parlour to the Library restaurant's haute cuisine (probably the most expensive in Britain); no possibility for design overlooked – from the carts in the Gallery restaurant by Marc Newson and the East Bar's toilet pods to the custom furniture pieces by Noe Duchaufour Lawrance. A total work of art for all the senses, Sketch sets new standards in the urban epicurean experience.

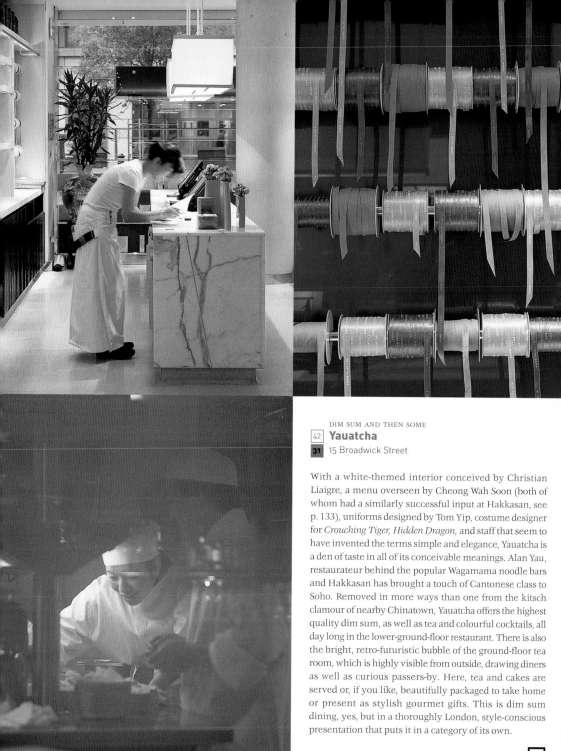

DIM SUM AND THEN SOME

42
Yauatcha

31 15 Broadwick Street

With a white-themed interior conceived by Christian Liaigre, a menu overseen by Cheong Wah Soon (both of whom had a similarly successful input at Hakkasan, see p. 133), uniforms designed by Tom Yip, costume designer for *Crouching Tiger, Hidden Dragon,* and staff that seem to have invented the terms simple and elegance, Yauatcha is a den of taste in all of its conceivable meanings. Alan Yau, restaurateur behind the popular Wagamama noodle bars and Hakkasan has brought a touch of Cantonese class to Soho. Removed in more ways than one from the kitsch clamour of nearby Chinatown, Yauatcha offers the highest quality dim sum, as well as tea and colourful cocktails, all day long in the lower-ground-floor restaurant. There is also the bright, retro-futuristic bubble of the ground-floor tea room, which is highly visible from outside, drawing diners as well as curious passers-by. Here, tea and cakes are served or, if you like, beautifully packaged to take home or present as stylish gourmet gifts. This is dim sum dining, yes, but in a thoroughly London, style-conscious presentation that puts it in a category of its own.

A CLASSIC REBORN

42 **Red Fort**

38 77 Dean Street

A shining example of high-style Indian cuisine – 'the Mother of Indian restaurants' it was dubbed by one publication in the know – even before its relaunch in 2000 (after being destroyed by a fire), what was once a classic has reinvented itself with an even greater commitment to contemporary cuisine, style and service. The recent reincarnation pays homage to the original Red Fort, built in Delhi by Shah Jahan, who also built the Taj Mahal, by incorporating the same materials but updated to contemporary demands in a lush and sultry setting. The menu is produced by chef Mohammed Rais, who comes from a 300-year line of court chefs and who has mastered the art of *dum pukht*, a form of steam cooking, which imbues regional biryanis with an added edge. A wide selection of refined dishes includes *dum ka* lobster, which has been steamed in cumin-infused broth, and *murgh mussalam*, poussin with Kashmiri chillies and browned onions. Downstairs is Akbar, much more than just a restaurant cocktail lounge.

INDIAN CUISINE REIMAGINED

14 **Zaika**

37 1 Kensington High Street

One of only two Indian restaurants in England to have achieved a Michelin star, Zaika is the winning marriage of restaurateur Claudio Pulze and prize-winning chef Vineet Bhatia. With its exotically inflected historic premises just off Hyde Park in Kensington, Zaika – which means 'sophisticated flavours' – presents classical dishes with new and inventive twists that are destined to redefine ethnic cuisine. The elegant setting of lush colours, contemporary Indian motifs and a stylish bar, is an ideal accompaniment to the refined dishes. Despite the departure of head chef Vineet Bhatia to open his own eponymous eatery (see p. 143) Zaika continues to maintain an unusually high standard of Indian cuisine. Choose from the *Jugalbandi* (or 'tasting') menu of five courses, or the nine-course 'Zaika Gourmand'. A la carte mains include *kesari jalpari*, tandoori monkfish and curry leaf risotto and *samundar machli*, roasted cod with crispy squid. For an extra charge of £10 wines will be matched with each course.

DELHI STAR

28 **Rasoi Vineet Bhatia**

14 10 Lincoln Street

Delhi-trained chef Vineet Bhatia brought the status of Indian food up a notch with Zaika (see p. 142), where he earned the place a Michelin star in 2001, the first ever for an Indian chef. It was an accomplishment he set out to achieve since arriving in London in 1993 as a trained chef and finding the state of Indian cooking here rather disappointing. In 2004 he left Zaika and moved to these premises, where the rooms are more intimate, the décor more luscious and the menu resembles poetry. Once on the plate, the choices aren't any less lyrical. The name translates to 'Vineet Bhatia's kitchen', and it is proudly a family operation, with Bhatia's wife, Rashima, running the dining room, which only seats 35. Upstairs, two small private dining rooms are available, one of which includes a roof terrace. Bhatia claims to have accomplished his dream in having his own restaurant in which to continue refining and experimenting with his native cuisine. You can also enjoy his cooking on British Airways First or Business Class flights.

Located a stone's throw from Smithfield Market, where livestock was traded for some 200 years, St John is a symbol of the British love affair with meat. This association, according to Trevor Gulliver, who started the restaurant with chef Fergus Henderson in 1994, happened somewhat by accident. True, one of the most famous and photographed items on their menu is bone marrow served with toasted flat bread and parsley salad, but this is more a reflection of the quality of the cuisine than a commitment to meat-eating. But St John also prides itself on its relationship with farmer-producers. Their fresh-baked bread can be bought from the bakery and the fact that they butcher their own meat gives them the opportunity and, they feel, an obligation to use all the parts. With a staunchly loyal following that includes dozens who ask for the menu to be faxed to them daily (some just so they can find out when tripe is being served), it is not hard to be won over by Gulliver's belief that 'a good restaurant is like a good friend'. The stark, whitewashed premises – which included a former smokehouse – complement the food perfectly.

28 **Tom Aikens**

5 43 Elystan Street

With a television documentary chronicling the daily grind of running his own restaurant in pursuit of at least one Michelin star, Tom Aikens seemed to run the risk of eclipsing his own gastronomic achievements with the entertainment value of personal struggle. But no need to worry. Though we may have seen one too many kitchen-confidential shows, what Tom Aikens really dishes out is worth talking about. From the black-painted façade on a Chelsea side street to the crisply white-clad waiters and simple floral displays, the feeling is one of serene sophistication. Of course, the menu follows suit, promising things that sound only mildly exotic but tempting enough and delivering a range of carefully crafted flavours that give credence to that Michelin rating. Choose duck foie gras and fig purée followed by turbot with langoustine ravioli or, if you're feeling more adventurous, the lauded braised pig's head with pork belly and stuffed trotter, and prepare for a memorable experience all around.

drink

When people think of London, they think of pubs. And while there are beautiful and characterful public houses throughout the city, those of great individual style are rare but well worth a detour. Today, however, pubs are only part of the story. Fuelled by London's famed club culture, its status as a magnet in the global design scene and more relaxed laws on drinking hours, chic watering holes are establishing themselves everywhere. After a couple of centuries of tea hegemony, coffee culture has re-entered London life, with delightful cafés popping up in neighbourhoods everywhere. Whether you're in the mood for a sleek lounge, a funky DJ dance-bar or an oak-panelled medieval pub — read on.

TEA WITH A VIEW
42 | The Portrait Restaurant
29 | The National Portrait Gallery, St Martin's Place

The National Portrait Gallery has always been one of London's must-see museums, but a recent extension and refurbishment have given it one of the best views in London. On top of the new Ondaatje wing, just behind the National Gallery on Trafalgar Square, the gallery's roof-top restaurant has magnificent views across London – the ideal place for an afternoon tea or late afternoon cocktail. With Nelson's Column rising up from a roofscape of white and verdigris domes, and Big Ben in the distance, the true drama of London's architecture is revealed in full.

VERY HIGH TEA
42 | The Drawing Room
26 | Brown's Hotel, 30–34 Albemarle Street

In 1837, the year Victoria became Queen of England, James Brown, a former valet to Lord Byron, decided to open a 'top class, genteel inn', which over the years has hosted British royalty, American presidents and a fair share of celebrities. It still displays its high Victorian charms, particularly in the delightfully indulgent ritual of afternoon tea. This is the apotheosis of English tea, with finger sandwiches, warm scones, clotted cream, decadent cakes and a selection of the world's finest blends, including Brown's own Afternoon Blend and 'flower infusions'.

BUCOLIC BANQUET

Inn the Park

St James's Park

Oliver Peyton, restaurateur founder of such swanky
London establishments as the Admiralty (p. 57) and Isola
(p. 155) has gone one better with Inn the Park, a stylish
restaurant set in the bucolic beauty of St James's Park,
overlooking the duck pond and just a stone's throw from
Buckingham Palace. The building by architect Michael
Hopkins and interior by Tom Dixon remind visitors that
they are in one of the most design-conscious cities in the
world. Good for high quality British food or just a drink
outside or up on the roof terrace.

A new take on the hotel bar, sensuously reimagined by designer David Collins, the Blue Bar takes the Regency interior to a new level of chic. Vivid blue – what Collins calls 'Lutyens blue' – and a white onyx bar and crocodile-leather print floor set the scene, with bull's-eye mirrors, Art Déco–style chairs and tasselled hanging lamps adding appropriate flourishes. Reflecting surfaces shine, as does the sparkling service. The cocktail selection, served with honeyed nuts, is civilized – no silly concoctions – mainly martinis, champagne cocktails and grown-up drinks.

If there ever was a truly down-to-earth wine bar, Gordon's is it. From 1364 it was a warehouse for cargoes of sherry and port coming off the busy River Thames. Its origins as a wine bar date from around 1870 and it has been in the hands of its current owner for more than 30 years. Today, you can still enjoy a glass of one of 80 wines in the subterranean medieval vaults that literally drip with ambience. The incomparable interiors, teeming with loyal customers (especially after work), bring alive another time that couldn't be recreated anywhere else.

For security reasons, you'll need to call in advance (one day for lunch, three weeks for evening drinks) to enjoy one of the most breathtaking views of London while sipping champagne. Curvy, bright-blue, swivelling armchairs take full advantage of the vistas from the 42nd floor, atop the tallest building in the City of London. Although the bar serves mainly champagne – 30 varieties at last count – there is a selection of wines as well as oysters, lobster, caviar and sushi. You pay for the view – but it's hard to imagine a better way to do so.

Ye Olde Mitre Tavern

Ely Place

The Mitre's history goes back to 1546 when it was built by Bishop Goodrich for the servants of Ely Palace. The palace appears in Shakespeare's *Richard II*, Doctor Johnson is said to have visited the tavern itself, and today you can still see the trunk of a cherry tree around which Queen Elizabeth is said to have danced on May Day. Probably the most attractive pub in London – and the hardest to find – the Mitre's small rooms and dark-wood panelling retain a pub atmosphere almost impossible to find elsewhere: no music, just the pleasing din of people chatting.

ART NOUVEAU PUB

86 The Blackfriar

1 174 Queen Victoria Street

Built on the site of a Dominican monastery that is today a rather unprepossessing concrete traffic interchange, the only Art Nouveau pub in a city dominated by Victoriana is an unexpected delight. Just across the Thames from the Tate Modern, the fantastic marble and gold-mosaiced 19th-century interior is largely overlooked, despite its curious and intimate 'grotto' (carved from a railway vault). The interior flourishes are made more appealing, perhaps, by the pub's pleasingly unprecious nature, as if it supposed all places should be like this.

WINE IN TRANSIT

72 Smithy's

17 15–17 Leeke Street

Off the busy, gritty travel hub of King's Cross, on a narrow cobblestoned alley in an emerging warehouse area, Smithy's barely makes itself known, but the unassuming exterior conceals one of the capital's most atmospheric wine bars. What used to be a 19th-century horse-drawn bus garage is the setting for a huge selection of wines by the glass or bottle, with light bar meals to soak up any excess. As the area around King's Cross is regenerating, so has a new owner at Smithy's tidied it up a bit, but the place's old character retains its charm.

14 **Windsor Castle**

32 114 Campden Hill Road

There's simply no modern way to create an interior that exudes the welcoming, gently time-worn ambience of the Windsor Castle, built in 1828, which appears to have remained virtually untouched for almost two centuries. Far from feeling rarefied, the pub – once an inn – seems as though it's always been an integral part of the quiet residential area in which it's set. While the deep wood atmosphere warms in winter, a large tree-shaded garden invites pleasurable drinking in summer. A place for quiet conversation or contemplation, whatever the season.

SHABBY GENTILITY

28 **Anglesea Arms**

7 15 Selwood Terrace

Just north of the shopping highway that is the Fulham Road, the Anglesea Arms sits in quiet repose, offering a welcoming embrace with outdoor tables in leafy shadows and a discreet period air that bespeaks the days when it was presented as a gift to Lady Joseph from her husband, Sir Maxwell Joseph. This is a pub whose early Victorian charms are well preserved, along with decorative details, such as framed old photographs and historic engravings, shaded chandeliers and velvet swag draperies that provide a reliably pleasing encounter every time.

Restaurateur Oliver Peyton has had a lot of hits over recent years, and Isola, a bar and restaurant, is one of them. Though the Italian with contemporary twists has plenty of draw, it is the ruby-red haven of handcrafted cocktails upstairs that provides the catalyst for designer drinking. Geometric-patterned wood surfaces, an over-dimensioned room with a floor-to-ceiling glass wall, red leather everywhere and retro chandeliers come together in an artful combination. Your evening begins here.

Cocktail bars don't really get much cooler than the Lonsdale. The Verner Panton décor, the members' bar, Genevieve, upstairs and the fact that you generally need to book ahead create an air of being among the select. Run by Henry Besant (formerly of the Sanderson), the Lonsdale is an arty, high-style backdrop to a high-flying drinks list that sets cocktail connoisseurs salivating. They cultivate a regular clientele with a 'guest list', which is by invitation only. But it's also possible to just go for a drink or two and soak up the atmosphere.

'Work should be play, because play is culture, culture is networking, networking is freedom and freedom is the best condition for working in,' so do Simon and Nicholas Kirkham describe the Westbourne Studios, a creative hive where small businesses and studios come together in a formerly derelict site under the A40 motorway. A catalyst in this interaction is Under the Westway, a hip bar and restaurant where people from the studios and the public can mingle, network, hang out or see one of the performances or exhibitions that fill the space.

Just off Old Street, Dragon Bar suggests its artistic origins and insider inclinations in details like the boxy concrete portico with discreet lettering on the bottom step and graffiti-splattered lavatories. Inside, a house DJ spins a rock-funky mix, sofas and chairs are strewn around seemingly at random. Against the sea of bars for the after-work crowd that are encroaching on Shoreditch's creative vibe, the Dragon is resolutely bohemian ('no office clothes'). For some this requires a leap of faith; for others, this is, and has been, the real thing.

Named after the brothels that were once sought out by sailors in port, not completely without meaning in this area of King's Cross, the Ruby Lounge has accomplished the somewhat contradictory task of making a rundown area more inviting. Along the ramshackle collection of improving and crumbling shopfronts, the Ruby Lounge's glowing red logo outside and breathtaking Verner Panton chandelier and wall lights inside are welcome signs in the night. The music is groovy, as are the people.

From its origins as a migrating Sunday afternoon dance club to one of the happiest venues in the West End, The Social is a product of the Heavenly record and club producers, whose parties have seen some of London's most famous DJs. In 1999, David Adjaye, architect of choice for London's Brit Artists, remodelled the interiors using unconventional exterior materials to create a two-level space that allows for all variety of dance activity. Add to that exceptionally clued-in music and a joyful crowd, and you've found your haven.

Under the arches of the Kingsland Viaduct, Cargo has taken on an ambitious task of providing restaurant, bar and club beneath a series of vaulted roofs and making them all seem very cool. With vague dockside theme, the branded Cargo logo greets you but that is the only given here. The open dining area is filled with giant square wood tables and views out to the planted courtyard garden. Music is one of the principal draws, with regular performances and internationally renowned DJs making the scene.

New bars come and go but in this area of Notting Hill a new venue that is trendy but friendly, noteworthy but welcoming is something to be pleased about. Sitting a mere stone's throw from the Electric Cinema (p. 19) and in the heart of the market shopping district, Trailer Happiness offers a comfortable kitschy atmosphere with tropical-themed décor and drinks to match. Its trailer-home vibe and cocktails, created by drinks guru Jonathan Downey (who launched the Matchbar) attract interested locals and hipsters alike.

Hoxton Square

- Bluu Bar, no. 1
- Hoxton Square Bar and Kitchen, nos 2–4
- Electricity Showrooms, no. 39A
- Liquid, 8 Pitfield Street
- Medicine Bar, 89 Great Eastern Street
- Great Eastern Dining Rooms, 54–56 Great Eastern St

Well within the last decade, Hoxton Square has become synonymous with hip art and craft studios during the daytime and groovy bars at night, largely supplanting Soho as a night-time destination. Inevitably, with the discovery of the area, many of the creatives who made the area what it is have moved on – but the vibe, day and night, remains intact, if made up more of visitors than with locals. Interestingly, most of the places that formed the early night life are still there, and still draw a crowd. Slightly off the square, a large, minimally furnished space with plate-glass windows, aglow with neon, announces what used to be electricity showrooms but has been for the last several years one of the area's principal watering holes. With a prominent but not prepossessing position on the south-west corner of Hoxton Square is Bluu, formerly the Blue Note club, which many would argue was the epicentre of drum 'n' bass dance music. Five years later it features a modern stainless-steel-trimmed interior and DJs who continue the tradition of its predecessor. Next door and down one level, this time lacking in signage, is the Hoxton Square Bar and Kitchen, another of the area's standbys. The open interior, set slightly below ground level, is animated at night by the eerie sensation of car headlights as they turn just before the bar. A few blocks away is Liquid, a small but vividly coloured venue that comes alive at night. Heading somewhat south to Great Eastern Street are Medicine Bar, and the Great Eastern Dining Rooms, which in addition to its bar and downstairs lounge serves respectable pan-Asian food.

shop

Like most metropolises, London is a hive of commercial activity, buzzing with grand department stores, stylish international-label outlets and off-beat boutiques. At the other end of the style spectrum are the dozens of street markets where real Londoners sell everything from antiques to country produce. Energized by the capital's renowned design schools, boutiques and speciality shops are springing up around the city – but are often off the beaten track. To understand what London style is all about, you need to seek the individualists who keep London on the global fashion map. For classic British labels or unheard-of street-chic upstarts, here is a guide.

Since she made her first collection of brocade mules in 1985, Emma Hope has won a number of design awards, including several from the Design Council, as well as one from *Harper's and Queen*. It is not hard to see why her lovingly detailed shoes should have garnered so much praise. Apart from fine leathers, Emma Hope shoes are made in such luxurious materials as nappa, suede, silk velvet, embroidered brocade and grosgrain, all designed by her and fabricated in Florence. Elegant and craftsmanlike, Hope has expanded her range to complementary bags.

A Cornish farm boy who learned the bootmaking craft, John Lobb received a royal warrant for his work from Edward, Prince of Wales, later Edward VII. Today the company holds three royal warrants from the Queen, the Duke of Edinburgh and the current Prince of Wales. The shop is a shrine to craftsmanship, as John Lobb still specialize in and have become almost synonymous with the art of the hand-made shoe. Each pair is numbered and fitted with its own shoe trees. Buckskin, satin calf and ostrich are just some of the leathers available.

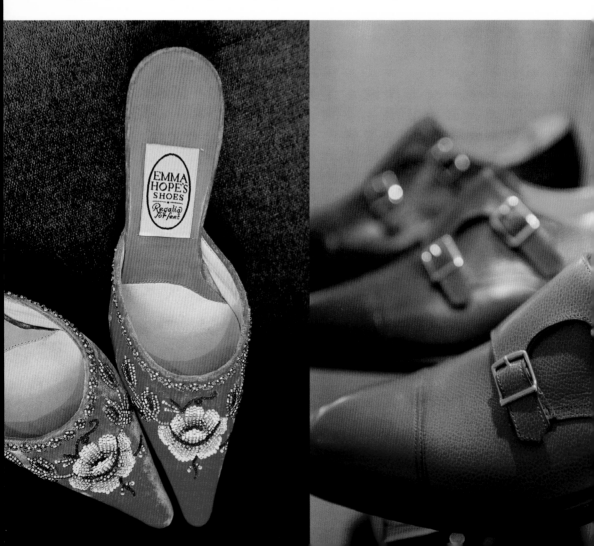

28 Manolo Blahník

 49–51 Old Church Street

Manolo Blahník's gold-accented shop is a must-see for any lover of footwear, with dramatic displays that raise shoes to the level of art objects, and many are just that, as his customers around the world are fully aware – Madonna says they're 'better than sex'. There is a high degree of concept, design and craftsmanship behind each pair of 'Manolos', the last for which the Canary Islands–born designer carves himself. Leathers are dyed in bright contrasting colours like pink and yellow or turquoise and lime. Despite his now firmly established fame, since first being 'discovered' by legendary fashion editor Diana Vreeland in 1970 and more recently brought into public consciousness by *Sex And The City*, Blahník is still the perfectionist who controls every aspect of the design and manufacture, and his first store in Chelsea is the place to find the genuine article.

12 Westbourne House, 122 Kensington Park Road

Starting out as a gopher in a clothing warehouse at 18, Paul Smith has gone on to become probably England's best-known menswear designer. Though he still has a solid reputation for cool elegance in men's fashion, particularly in Japan, in England his presence is comparatively slight. Since branching into women's and children's wear and home fashion, his original shop in Covent Garden (p. 54) has been somewhat superseded by the design emporium at Westbourne House in Notting Hill. Living the designer's dream, Smith obtained a large, double-fronted Victorian corner house and filled it with his personal vision, which consists of the full range of his clothing and home ware, as well as his first bespoke tailoring service. Paul Smith may be widely available, but the Westbourne House experience feels like a glimpse into his private world.

Paul Smith

The most famous street for men's suits in the world needs no introduction, but times have changed, and the prevailing trend to modernize classics is influencing the look on Savile Row. Led by innovators such as Ozwald Boateng (p. 166), a generation of ever-so-slightly daring or even irreverent younger tailors are beginning to seize control. Amid the highly traditional shops are edgier talents, such as Richard James, who has been honoured by the British Fashion Council and has attracted a younger clientele with his modern cuts and banned advertisements. For a glimpse back in time, peek into the timeless office of age-old Anderson & Sheppard, who are perhaps best known for dressing royalty and where British fashion star Alexander McQueen cut his cloth as a teenager. William Hunt's sartorial flair has won him a number of music-world clients.

BESPOKE MASTERY
42 **Ozwald Boateng**
8 9 Vigo Street

No one in recent years has caused a stir in 'traditional' men's fashion quite like Ozwald Boateng. Taking his cue from classic British men's suits, Boateng has injected a certain exoticism and a flair for cut and colour that have utterly transformed the quintessential jacket and trousers while retaining their integrity. Tones, patterns and fabrics that might have once been sniffed at have attained new levels of acceptability in Boateng's 'bespoke couture' collection. His suits are among the most sought-after in London – for those well-dressed who dare to be different.

ONE-STOP ULTRASHOP
42 **Selfridges**
4 400 Oxford Street

Selfridges used to be a massive store with an impressive façade housing a rambling not particularly impressive set of concessions. Enter Vittorio Radice in 1996, whose experience as international buyer at Habitat put him in touch with a design-savvy public hungry for novel retail environments. Radice revivified the ailing giant, reinvented a number of departments, refurbished the entire store and brought in new labels, talent, look and vibe. Now Selfridges redefines 'one-stop' shopping for a new, discerning generation of consumers.

- Harvie & Hudson, no. 97
- Turnbull & Asser, nos 71–72
- J. Floris, no. 89
- Dunhill, no. 48

The street of men's shirtmakers is a must-see for anyone looking to procure the genuine English article, from shoes to shirts. Harvie & Hudson, which was founded in 1929, is at no. 97, and even if their traditional style is not to your liking, the fine Victorian shopfront is worth the short walk from any of the numerous establishments. Dunhill, now available worldwide, started out as Alfred Dunhill the tobacconist before becoming the global purveyor of fine menswear and accessories, today with a decidedly modern edge. Provisions of a different sort are available at J. Floris, the oldest perfumer in London, established as a barber shop in 1730 by Juan Famenias Floris of Menorca. The shop's interior is bejewelled with the bottled essences, candles, soaps and lotions, some displayed in the Spanish mahogany cabinets that were obtained from the Great Exhibition of 1852. For shirts, it must be Turnbull & Asser, probably the street's best-known shop, which also features bespoke shirts. Fine mother-of-pearl buttons, specially woven Sea Island cotton, 'the most gentlemanly of shirtings', and broad, three-buttoned cuffs are among Turnbull & Asser's trademarks.

Eley Kishimoto has become one of the hottest names in London fashion, being both known to the fashion aware and yet unknown, as so little about them has been publicized. Mark Eley and his Japanese wife, Wakako Kishimoto, both trained in England. They took over this former jam factory in Bermondsey, which serves as their workshop, factory and only public showroom, though their designs are sold through other outlets worldwide. Known for their unique printed designs, which are mostly hand-drawn by Kishimoto and applied to everything from textiles to luggage to wallpaper, the two got their start producing patterns for top designers such as Alexander McQueen (see p. 173), Nicole Farhi and Hussein Chalayan. They then began producing their own ready-to-wear collections twice a year, and have been consistently successful with their striking designs that border tantalizingly on the kitsch. Accessible to more than just the fashion élite, they are certainly set for bigger things, so get them while you can.

DESIGN BY ORDER
42 Oki-Ni
9 25 Savile Row

Oki-Ni is a high-concept store, not just in the sense of offering a range of products aimed at a particular design 'lifestyle', but in that you cannot actually take anything away from the shop. Everything from trousers and trainers to jackets and tops is there to be ordered through oki-ni.com. This is no clearing house for designer gear, however, the London-based design group works in collaboration with select brands and clothes designers to create items that are produced in limited numbers, all of it unique to Oki-Ni and only available online from their website. Designers for their exclusive range include Adidas, Evisu, Levis®, Fake London, Cockfighter, Dennis Morris, Motorola and Paul Smith. So while the satisfaction of actually walking away with a one-off piece in hand is not there, the knowledge that you are getting something very special and possibly unique is, even if you have to wait for it to arrive in the post.

86 **Lara Bohinc 107**

20 51 Hoxton Square

Cameron Diaz, Björk, Lucy Liu and Sarah Jessica Parker are among the A-list celebrities who have fallen under the spell of Lara Bohinc's cutting-edge, but distinctly feminine jewelry pieces. Until recently, Bohinc's creations were available only through large luxury retailers, but in late 2004 the young, Slovenian-born designer opened her only shop in the creative hub of Hoxton Square. Now her Drops collection, inspired by the designs of the 1920s and 1930s, Ovals, is a new take on modern classics and Curb collection, which draws on the hip-hop urban influences, are all available in one space.

14 **Dinny Hall**

27 200 Westbourne Grove

Despite the appearance of her pieces in the fashion press and the roster of high-profile clients, there is something pleasingly understated about Dinny Hall jewelry. The lines are simple and the cuts of precious and semiprecious stones correspondingly elegant. Hall's status as a top British designer was confirmed when she was commissioned to design a line for the new Tate Modern when it opened in 2000. The jewelry is handmade in the studio just behind the Westbourne Grove shop, and the prices are almost ridiculously reasonable given her universal appeal and demand.

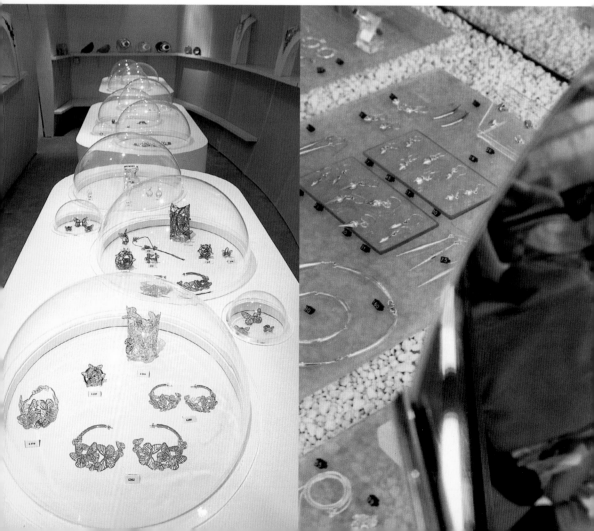

Irishman Philip Treacy's approach to millinery is that of a sculptor. He staged the first catwalk show of his own designs in 1993 with the help of supermodels Christy Turlington, Kate Moss and Naomi Campbell. But Treacy's designs are worth the attention on their own, whether it's a pale pink top hat set off with a giant silk rose, a proliferation of green leaves sprouting from a headband or a delicate swirl perched atop a well-groomed forehead. And while he designs for some of the most exclusive customers, he also makes a not-so-haute range, available in this shop, that lesser mortals can enjoy.

Westbourne Grove is chock-a-block with designer boutiques, but this gem of a bespoke jewelry shop is slightly removed from the fray. Despite the ruby-red front, it doesn't announce itself, and though you are welcome to drop in, you must make an appointment if you want a consultation with the lady herself. Having worked for costume jewelers Butler & Wilson (see p. 32), Azagury-Partridge is one of Britain's most inventive jewelry designers, whose bold, baroque creations in 18 carat yellow, white and rose gold and platinum are full of shape, colour and wit.

Stella McCartney

30 Bruton Street

Rising from the ranks of young British fashion designers, McCartney became a star in her own right – despite her famous family name – as head of fashion house Chloe and creator of her own widely respected label. Her first stellar boutique opened in New York, showing just how quickly she has gained international appeal for her clothes, which often combine loose and baggy elements with close-fitting cuts – little feminine twists, a blousy shoulder, a flying cuff, a tuck in just the right place – to draw attention to the form beneath the fashion. The new Bruton Street shop is almost as beautifully detailed as McCartney's creations. The Georgian period townhouse has been restored with grand spaces and period elements lightened up with a glass-covered atrium leading to the shoe room, where the sexy-funky footwear features the label 'suitable for vegetarians'. Wood floors, a dainty woodland motif wall covering, plum-coloured carpet leading up a spiral stair to more airy rooms, and a boudoir space hung with lingerie and dotted with jewel-like perfume bottles is an enchanting display that doesn't upstage the items on sale.

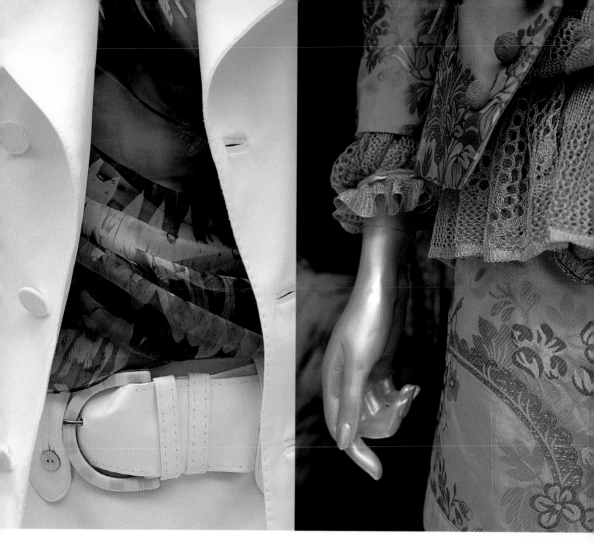

THE WOW FACTOR

 Alexander McQueen

21 4–5 Old Bond Street

Once the bad-boy of British fashion, now one of the world's leading fashion designers, Alexander McQueen has been stirring things up since his entire degree collection was bought by fashion patron Isabella Blow in 1995. Beginning as an apprentice to Savile Row tailors at the age of sixteen, McQueen moved on to work with theatrical costumiers and learn pattern-cutting by going back to designs from the 16th century. After a five-year stint as chief designer for Givenchy, he turned his focus to his own label, opening his exclusive shops and developing a menswear line, eyeglasses and signature fragrance. He is known almost as well for his theatrical catwalk shows as he is for the clothes that deliberately combine old with new, subtle lines with dramatic gestures and 'brutally sharp tailoring'. This shop, opened in 2003 (the year he was also awarded a CBE) is a dynamic backdrop for the visual and textural excitement that is McQueen's trademark and has won him a list of celebrity clients, not to mention a place among fashion royalty.

David Mellor operates on the simple principle that well-designed equipment can improve your life. Mellor, Royal Designer for Industry, has an international reputation. He has always specialized in metalwork and has often been described as 'the cutlery king'. Mellor opened his Sloane Square shop in 1969. Today it sells his own range of tableware and a large selection of kitchen accessories, as well as his cutlery range in silver plate and stainless steel, all manufactured in England.

Located in edgy Ladbroke Grove opposite Myro Goldfinger's brutalist triumph (or terror, some might say), Trellik Tower, Rellik is a second-hand shop with a difference, as its loyal customers and fashion-magazine editors are well aware. Three former Portobello Road stall owners set up shop to offer select vintage wear from the 1920s onward, each with her own area of speciality, including both ready-to-wear and couture pieces. If you look hard enough, you might just find a classic Westwood outfit.

60 **Gallery 1930/Susie Cooper Ceramics**

1 18 Church Street

Probably London's most comprehensive collection of Art Déco ceramics, furniture and lighting is housed in a small but richly filled shop on a road that is like a secret hoard of antiques dealers. Alfie's, a collection of dealers' stalls, has been going for years. Geoffrey Peake and Nick Jones first set up shop at Alfie's as Susie Cooper Ceramics, selling mostly the work of the 'quintessentially English designer', who began working in the 1920s. In their own premises they offer a wide collection of 1930s pieces, including boldly patterned Clarice Cliff vessels and solid-hued Keith Murray designs for Wedgwood.

14 **Bill Amberg**

21 10 Chepstow Road

If you love leather the way Bill Amberg loves leather then you will love just about everything he does. His affinity for the stuff means that he doesn't make dainty strappy accessories but things that you can run your hand over, smell or walk on. From cowhide leather floors to vellum for a drawer liner, he expertly works each kind to its advantage. His women's bags are ample and luxuriously free of fussy details, as are his men's modern but supple cases and accessories. Attention is given to shape and to the smooth finish, texture and deep colours.

retreat

It is probably true that the real England is in the country, not in the cities. And though the regions immediately surrounding London's concrete jungle are in many ways bucolic translations of the city sensibility, it is not hard to find pockets — by the sea, in the countryside, in villages — that feel worlds away, even though some are a mere 30 minutes by train from the city. These four getaways represent very different experiences, but each is distinctly English and an ideal tonic after an intoxicating few days in the urban buzz.

Brighton: Seaside Hip
- Blanch House
- Hotel Pelirocco

Formerly the playground of Regency royals and today a hip seaside clubbing destination, Brighton is the quintessential English getaway, particularly for the youthfully inclined. Dynamized by students from the local university, one of the liveliest nightclub scenes in the the UK, if not Europe, the recreation destination is just over an hour from London. An unusually high concentration of record and jewelry shops, quarters of narrow pedestrianized lanes and the wide-open boardwalk unite in a cool concoction of kitsch, fun, craft and decadence.

The town centre has four principal quarters: North Laine, a tight grid of quaint, brightly coloured houses with lively boutiques and bars; the Lanes, a rabbit warren of even narrower alleyways packed with clothes shops and jewelers; the Seafront, which features a boardwalk and the Arches, a long colonnade comprising mainly restaurants and bars, many of which turn into nightclubs when day becomes night; and Kemp Town, east of the pier, between St James Street and Marina Drive, with a more relaxed vibe.

At opposite ends of the action, are two hotels whose character fits perfectly with the Brighton scene. Blanch House, a delightful 12-room hotel opened in 2000 by Amanda Blanch and Chris Edwardes in Kemp Town, is intimate, with each room quirkily themed and cleverly decorated; its small restaurant serves contemporary British. Hotel Pelirocco, on Regency Square, is all rock 'n' roll (without the volume): Playstations in every room, idiosyncratic decoration and a host of guests from London's music scene have garnered the hotel international attention and a colourful following.

For a relatively small town, there is a high concentration of shops, over 300 at last count, many of which are independently owned and feature a broad spectrum of wares, from streetwear and locally designed crafts to 1970s furniture and decorative objects, to kites and beachwear – with prices generally noticeably lower than their London counterparts. Do not miss the Royal Pavilion, a faux-exotic pleasure palace built by George IV in 1785 as a residence – an entirely appropriate symbol of the town's exuberance and excess.

Bath and Babington House: Georgian Splendour, Contemporary Style
Somerset

Londoners have been going to Bath for rest and rejuvenation probably since the Romans first exploited the natural hot springs. But it was at the height of popularity as a retreat for the fashionable rich during the 18th century, when English architects John Wood and Son created the elegant neo-classical squares and crescents using golden Bath stone, making it one of the most picturesque cities in England – today just over an hour by train from London. The city's heart is the convergence of the Abbey Church (1616), the Roman Baths and Museum and the Pump Room, a grand 18th-century tea-room that gives something of the flavour of Bath society popularized by Jane Austen. In the elevated north-west near the park and botanic gardens, the Royal Crescent is a masterpiece of 18th-century architecture.

Restaurants and lodgings are abundant in Bath but a stylish and fitting base is just a few miles away, near Frome, in the early Georgian country estate of Babington House where 18th-century charm and modern convenience have been married to fruitful success. Nick Jones, the enterprising figure behind the Soho Club and the refurbished Electric Cinema (p. 19) in London, has brought modern comforts – such as a heated outdoor swimming pool, a cinema, clubby bar (try the house champagne cocktail or hot toddy) and gourmet restaurant – to a discerning urban crowd and nestled them comfortably in the arms of this grand country house. Drawing rooms with furniture by contemporary designers and rustic-chic room décor that respect the architecture have transformed the manor house into a very singular environment. With gym and spa facilities housed in a former cowshed, which overlooks the two lap pools, the picture is complete. Everything is perfectly in keeping with Bath's history as a place of high fashion: there is nothing that Georgian aristocrats wouldn't expect to find, were they cavorting here in the 21st century. The large light-filled breakfast room offers meals almost any time of day and the restaurant delivers high-quality dishes that take full advantage of local and organic produce.

Bray: an Epicurean Destination

- The Waterside Inn
- The Fat Duck
- The Hind's Head
- Monkey Island Hotel

A mere 30-minute train journey from Paddington station takes you to one of the highest concentrations of Michelin stars in the country, set in the verdant Thames-side setting of Bray, a 16th-century village. Just a few minutes apart, The Waterside Inn and The Fat Duck, both in converted country pubs, have set the highest standards in culinary excellence – in completely different ways.

The Waterside Inn was opened by Albert and Michel Roux, the brothers who in 1967 redefined London's world of gastronomy with the opening of Le Gavroche. Today Michel and his son Alain, who recently assumed the helm to rave reviews, run the Waterside Inn with the élan and elegance that have made it another modern institution. Despite the excellence of the food and service, the converted pub surroundings and dining room overlooking the river impart a notably unstuffy air – formality softened by countryside.

Pursuing excellence in a very different manner, The Fat Duck is the product of Heston Blumenthal. Since opening the restaurant in 1995, he has explored innovative modes of cooking that draw on science rather than conventional kitchen methods. His intensive research into chemistry, psychology and sensory perception – an approach sometimes referred to as 'molecular gastronomy' – has uncovered an unexpected spectrum of tastes, moods and memories that are a revolution in cooking. More recently, Blumenthal has applied his chemical wizardry to classic pub-style comfort food at the nearby Hind's Head, an ideal alternative for those seeking a less formal meal in warm surroundings.

After such splendid dining experiences, you will want nothing more than to fall asleep to the sound of the Thames lapping against its banks. For those too sated to move, the Waterside Inn offers 10 rooms in the main house and outbuildings around the site. On a tiny Thames island close to both restaurants, the peaceful Monkey Island Hotel is a historical property accessed only by a pedestrian bridge. Most of its 26 rooms have river or garden views.

Gravetye Manor:
The Quintessential Country House Experience
East Grinstead, West Sussex

Less than 30 miles south-west of London, a thousand acres of forest are the setting for one of the south-east's most luxurious country-house hotels. After a 50-minute train ride from central London you arrive in the Sussex town of East Grinstead; a short taxi drive takes you through green countryside to historic Gravetye Manor. Built in 1598 by Richard Infield for his wife, Katherine, the stone mansion retains most of its Elizabethan elements, despite periods of neglect. Some of the windows are still ornamented with delicate wrought-iron glazing bars and open to the expanse of gardens and fields that were tamed and encouraged by a renowned English landscape gardener, William Robinson.

Robinson bought the manor and the surrounding land in 1884 and lived there until he died in 1935, laying out the gardens of small plants and flowers, trees and shrubs, and pioneering what became known as the English 'natural' style. The arrangement of the gardens is his living legacy and no small part of the appeal of Gravetye, which was bought by Peter Herbert and converted to a hotel in 1958.

The interiors are enchanting. Warm wood rooms, printed English fabrics, period portraits and flowers, as well as service that is informal but highly discreet and attentive, make guests feel truly welcome in an atmosphere of old-world luxury. Two wood-panelled drawing rooms, each with a well-tended wood fire, can be used by guests for quiet reading, relaxing or for having tea or drinks. The restaurant, led by chef Mark Raffan, has earned a Michelin star, so requires booking ahead. Around lunch you might consider a walk through the countryside to the rustic pub of a neighbouring village.

Rooms are finely decorated in traditional English style, even with the occasional ceiling or floor slant that is so much part of the character of this cherished old property. Peter and Susan Herbert strive to maintain an air that is 'not trendy but at the same time not aged and stuffy'. Their 40 years of experience with the house and the clientele ensure that their delightful establishment will continue for many years.

contact

All telephone numbers are given for dialling locally: the country code for England is 44; the city code for London 20. Calling from abroad, therefore, one dials (+44 20) plus the number given below. Telephone numbers in the retreat section are given for dialling from London: if calling from abroad, dial the country code (44) and drop the 0 at the start of the number. The number in brackets by the name is the page number on which the entry appears.

Adam Street [135]
9 Adam Street
London WC2N 6AA
T   7379 8000
F   7379 1444
E   reception@adamstreet.co.uk
W   www.adamstreet.co.uk

The Admiralty [57]
Somerset House, Strand
London WC2R 1LA
T   7845 4646
W   www.somerset-house.org.uk

Alexander McQueen [173]
4–5 Old Bond Street
London W1S 4PD
T   7355 0088
W   www.alexandermcqueen.co.uk

Almeida Theatre [81]
Almeida Street
London N1 1TA
T   7359 4404
W   www.almeida.co.uk

Amphitheatre Café & Restaurant [54]
Royal Opera House, Covent Garden
London WC2E 9DD
T   7212 9254
F   7212 9239
E   searcys@roh.org.uk
W   www.royalopera.org

Anchor & Hope [102]
36 The Cut
London SE1 8LP
T   7928 9898

Anderson & Sheppard Ltd [165]
30 Savile Row
London W1S 3PT
T   7734 1420
F   7734 1721

Anglesea Arms [154]
15 Selwood Terrace
London SW7 3QG
T   7373 7960

Annie's [81]
12 Camden Passage
London N1 8ED
T   7359 0796
F   7359 2116

Antoni & Alison [74]
43 Rosebery Avenue
London EC1R 4SH
T F 7833 2002
E   info@antoniandalison.co.uk
W   www.antoniandalison.co.uk

Anya Hindmarch [37]
15–17 Pont Street
London SW1X 9EH
T   7838 9177
F   7838 9111
W   www.anyahindmarch.com

Anything Left-Handed [49]
57 Brewer Street
London W1F 9UL
T   7437 3910
W   www.anythingleft-handed.co.uk

aquaint [57]
38 Monmouth Street
London WC2H 9EP
T   7240 9677
F   7240 4209

Ashbells [20]
29 All Saints Road
London W11 1HE
T   7221 8585
E   info@ashbells-uk.com
W   www.ashbells-uk.com

Asprey [47]
167 New Bond Street
London W1S 4AY
T   7493 6767
F   7491 0384
W   www.asprey.com

@Work [90]
156 Brick Lane
London E1 6RU
T F 7377 0597
W   www.atworkgallery.com

Baby Ceylon [17]
Unit 16, Portobello Green Arcade
281 Portobello Road
London W10 5TZ
T   8968 9501

Baltic [101]
74 Blackfriars Road
London SE1 8HA
T   7928 1111
F   7928 8487
E   info@balticrestaurant.co.uk
W   www.balticrestaurant.co.uk

Bam-Bou [64]
1 Percy Street
London W1T 1DB
T   7323 9130
F   7323 9140
W   www.bam-bou.co.uk

Bed Bar [17]
310 Portobello Road
London W10 5TA
T   8969 4500

Ben Day [90]
18 Hanbury Street
London E1 6QR
T   7247 9977
E   info@benday.co.uk
W   www.benday.co.uk

Bermondsey Market [107]
Bermondsey Square
London SE1

Bibendum Oyster Bar [31]
Michelin House, 81 Fulham Road
London SW3 6RD
T   7589 1480
F   7823 7925
E   manager@bibendum.co.uk
W   www.bibendum.co.uk

Bill Amberg [175]
10 Chepstow Road
London W2 5BD
T   7727 3560
F   7727 3541
W   www.billamberg.com

The Blackfriar [153]
174 Queen Victoria Street
London EC4B 4EG
T   7236 5474

Blenheim Books [20]
11 Blenheim Crescent
London W11 2EE
T   7792 0777
E   sales@blenheimbooks.co.uk

Blue Bar [150]
The Berkeley Hotel, Wilton Place
London SW1X 7RL
T 7201 1680
F 7235 4330
W www.the-berkeley.co.uk

Bluu Bar [159]
1 Hoxton Square
London N1 6NU
T 7613 2793

Boiler House [90]
Brick Lane, opposite Truman Brewery
London E1

bookartbookshop [92]
17 Pitfield Street
London N1 6HB
T 7608 1333

Books for Cooks [20]
4 Blenheim Crescent
London W11 1NN
T 7221 1992
E booksforcooks.com
W www.booksforcooks.com

Boyd [37]
42 Elizabeth Street
London SW1W 9NZ
T 7730 3939

Brick Lane Beigel Bake [90]
159 Brick Lane
London E1 6TS
T 7729 0616

Browns + Browns Focus [44]
Browns: 23–27 South Molton Street
London W1K 5RD
Browns Focus: 38–39 South
   Molton Street
London W1K 5RN
T 7514 0000
F 7408 1281
W www.brownsfashion.com

Burlington Arcade [48]
Off Piccadilly
London W1
W www.burlington-arcade.co.uk

Burro [54]
29 Floral Street
London WC2E 9DP
T 7240 5120
F 7379 7465
E sales@burro.co.uk
W www.burro.co.uk

Butler & Wilson [32]
189 Fulham Road
London SW3 6JN
T 7352 3045
F 7376 5981
E info@butlerandwilson.co.uk
W www.butlerandwilson.co.uk

Butlers Wharf Chop House [105]
The Butlers Wharf Building
36e Shad Thames
London SE1 2YE
T 7403 3403
F 7403 3414
W www.conran-restaurants.co.uk

Cadogan London [116]
75 Sloane Street
London SW1X 9SG
T 7235 7141
F 7245 0994
W www.cadogan.com

Café 1001 [90]
Dray Walk, Brick Lane
London E1

Canal [82]
42 Cross Street
London N1 2BA
T 7704 0222

Cantina del Ponte [105]
The Butlers Wharf Building
36c Shad Thames
London SE1 2YE
T 7403 5403
F 7403 4432
W www.conran-restaurants.co.uk

Cargo [158]
83 Rivington Street
London EC2A 3AY
T 7739 3440
F 7739 3441
W www.cargo-london.com

Carhartt [51]
13 Newburgh Street
London W1F 7RS
T 7287 6411

Caroline Groves [63]
37 Chiltern Street
London W1U 7PW
T 7935 2329
W www.carolinegroves.co.uk

Cath Kidston [18]
8 Clarendon Cross
London W11 4AP
T 7221 4000
F 7229 1992
W www.cathkidston.co.uk

Chelsea Physic Garden [35]
66 Royal Hospital Road
London SW3 4HS
T 7352 5646
F 7376 3910
W www.chelseaphysicgarden.co.uk

Christ Church, Spitalfields [90]
Commercial Street
London E1 6QE
T 7247 0165

Cinch [51]
5 Newburgh Street
London W1V 1LH
T 7287 4941
F 7287 6496

Cinnamon Club [139]
30 Great Smith Street
London SW1P 3BU
T 7222 2555
F 7222 1333
E info@cinnamonclub.com
W www.cinnamonclub.com

Claridge's [47]
55 Brook Street
London W1A 2JQ
T 7629 8860
F 7499 2210
E info@claridges.co.uk
W www.claridges.co.uk

Coco de Mer [57]
23 Monmouth Street
London WC2H 9DD
T 7836 8882
F 7836 8881
W www.coco-de-mer.co.uk

**Columbia Road Flower
Market** [94]
Columbia Road
London E2
W www.Columbia-flower-
   market.freewebspace.com
Sunday mornings 8 am–2 pm

Comfort & Joy [82]
109 Essex Road
London N1 2FL
T 7359 3898

Contemporary Applied Arts [66]
2 Percy Street
London W1T 1DD
T 7436 2344
F 7436 2446
W www.caa.org.uk

Cornelissen & Son [68]
105 Great Russell Street
London WC1B 3RY
T 7636 1045
F 7636 3655
E info@cornelissen.co.uk
W www.cornelissen.co.uk

Couverture [32]
310 King's Road
London SW3 5UH
T 7795 1200
F 7795 1202
E info@couverture.co.uk
W www.couverture.co.uk

The Cow [138]
89 Westbourne Park Road
London W2 5QH
T 7221 5400

Crafts Council [79]
44a Pentonville Road
London N1 9BY
T 7278 7700
F 7837 6891
W www.craftscouncil.org.uk

The Cross [18]
141 Portland Road
London W11 4LR
T 7727 6760
F 7727 6745

Cross Street Gallery [82]
40 Cross Street
London N1 2BA
T 7226 8600

The Crown [79]
116 Cloudesley Road
London N1 0EB
T 7837 7107
F 7833 1084
E crown.islington@fullers.co.uk

Cutler & Gross [38]
16 Knightsbridge Green
London SW1X 7QL
T 7581 2250
F 7584 5702
Cutler and Gross Vintage:
7 Knightsbridge Green
London SW1X 7QL
T 7590 9995
F 7590 9995
W www.cutlerandgross.co.uk

CVO Firevault [64]
36 Great Titchfield Street
London W1W 8BQ
T 7580 5333
F 7255 2234

E enquiries@cvofirevault.co.uk
W www.cvo.co.uk

Daunt Books [63]
83–84 Marylebone High Street
London W1U 4QW
T 7224 2295

David Mellor [174]
4 Sloane Square
London SW1W 8EE
T 7730 4259
F 7730 7240
W www.davidmellordesign.com

Delfina [106]
50 Bermondsey Street
London SE1 3UD
T 7357 0244
W www.delfina.org.uk

Dennis Severs's House [89]
18 Folgate Street
London E1 6BX
T 7247 4013
F 7377 5548
E info@dennissevershouse.co.uk
W www.dennissevershouse.co.uk

Design Mueseum [107]
28 Shad Thames
London SE1 2YD
T 7940 8790
E showroom@designersguild.com
W www.designmuseum.org

Designers' Guild [32]
267 and 277 King's Road
London SW3 5EN
T 7351 5775
F 7243 7710
W www.designersguild.com

Designworks [52]
42–44 Broadwick Street
London W1F 7AE
T 7434 1968

Dinny Hall [170]
200 Westbourne Grove
London W11 2RH
T 7792 3913
F 7792 8322
E sales@dinnyhall.co.uk
W www.dinnyhall.com

The Dispensary [51]
9 Newburgh Street (womenswear)
London W1F 7RL
T 7287 8145
15 Newburgh Street (menswear)
London W1F 7RX
T 7734 4095
E info@thedispensary.net
W www.thedispensary.net

$ Grills and Martinis [77]
2 Exmouth Market
London EC1R 4PX
T 7278 0077

Dover Castle [63]
43 Weymouth Mews
London W1G 7EQ
T 7580 4412

Dragon Bar [156]
5 Leonard Street
London EC2A 4AQ
T 7490 7110

Draper's Arms [79]
44 Barnsbury Street

London N1 1ER
T 7619 0348

The Drawing Room [148]
Brown's Hotel,
30–34 Albemarle Street
London W1S 4BP
T 7493 6020
F 7493 9381
W www.brownshotel.com

dreambagsjaguarshoes [94]
34–36 Kingsland Road
London E2 8DA
T 7729 5830
W www.dreambagsjaguarshoes.com

Duchamp [23]
75 Ledbury Road
London W11 2AG
T 7243 3970
F 7243 4708
E admin@duchamp.co.uk
W www.duchamp.co.uk

Duke of Cambridge [79]
30 St Peters Street
London N1 8JT
T 7359 3066
W www.singhboulton.co.uk

The Duke (of York) [69]
7 Roger Street
London WC1N 2PB
T 7242 7230

Dunhill [167]
48 Jermyn Street
London SW1Y 6DL
T 7290 8602
W www.dunhill.com

The Eagle [138]
159 Farringdon Road
London EC1R 3AL
T 7837 1353
F 7689 5882

EC One [77]
41 Exmouth Market
London EC1R 4QL
T 7713 6185
F 7833 3151
W www.econe.co.uk

Egg [38]
36 Kinnerton Street
London SW1X 8EF
T 7235 9315
F 7838 9705
E egg@eggtrading.com

The Electric Cinema [19]
191 Portobello Road
London W11 2ED
T 7908 9696
F 7908 9595
W www.electriccinema.co.uk

Electricity Showrooms [159]
39A Hoxton Square
London N1 6NU
T 7739 6934
F 7739 6451

Eleven Cadogan Gardens [124]
11 Cadogan Gardens
London SW3 2RJ
T 7730 7000
F 7730 5217
E letterbox@number-eleven.co.uk
W www.number-eleven.co.uk

Eley Kishimoto [168]
40 Snowsfields
London SE1 3JQ
T 7357 0037
W www.eleykishimoto.com

Elk in the Woods [81]
39 Camden Passage
London N1 8AE
T 7226 3535

Elspeth Gibson [37]
7 Pont Street
London SW1X 9EJ
T 7235 0601
F 7235 0602
W www.elspethgibson.com

Emma Hope's Shoes [162]
207 Westbourne Grove
London W11 2SE
T 7313 7490
F 7313 7491
W www.emmahope.co.uk

Emmett London [32]
380 King's Road
London SW3 5UZ
T 7351 7529
F 7376 4231
4 Eldon Street
London EC2M 7LS
T 7247 1563
E info@emmettshirts.com
W www.emmettlondon.com

Estorick Collection [82]
39A Canonbury Square
London N1 2AN
T 7704 9522
F 7704 9531
E info@estorickcollection.com
W www.estorickcollection.com

Euphorium Bakery [81]
203 Upper Street
London N1 1RQ
T 7704 6909
F 7704 6089

Exmouth Grill [77]
55–57 Exmouth Market
London EC1R 4QL
T 7833 2026
W www.exmouthgrill.co.uk

Eyre Brothers [94]
70 Leonard Street
London EC2A 4QX
T 7613 5346
F 7739 8199
W www.eyrebrothers.co.uk

Family Tree [77]
53 Exmouth Market
London EC1R 4QL
T/F 7278 1084
E mail@familytreeshop.co.uk
W www.familytreeshop.co.uk

Fandango [82]
50 Cross Street
London N1 2BA
T/F 7226 1777
E shop@fandango.uk.com
W www.fandango.uk.com

Faraday Museum [49]
21 Albemarle Street
London W1S 4BS
T 7409 2992
F 7629 3569
W www.rigb.org

Fashion & Textile Museum [106]
83 Bermondsey Street
London SE1 3XF
T 7403 0222
F 7403 0555
E info@ftmlondon.org
W www.ftmlondon.org

Fino [64]
33 Charlotte Street
London W1
T 7813 8010

Fiona Knapp [23]
178A Westbourne Grove
London W11 2RH
T 7313 5941
E info@fionaknapp.com
W www.fionaknapp.com

Fish Shop on St John Street [79]
360–62 St John Street
London EC1V 4NR
T 7837 1199
E info@thefishshop.net
W www.thefishshop.net

Flow [23]
1–5 Needham Road
London W11 2RP
T 7243 0782
E info@flowgallery.co.uk
W www.flowgallery.co.uk

The Foundry [93]
84–86 Great Eastern Street
London EC2A 3JL
T 7739 6900
W www.foundry.tv

Frederick's [81]
106 Camden Passage
London N1 8EG
T 7359 2888
F 7359 5173
E eat@fredericks.co.uk
W www.fredericks.co.uk

The French House [51]
49 Dean Street
London W1D 5BG
T 7437 2477
F 7287 9109

Gagosian Gallery [81]
6–24 Britannia Street
London WC1X 9JP
T 7841 9960
8 Heddon Street
London W1B 4BU
T 7292 8222
E info@gagosian.com
W www.gagosian.com

Gallery 1930/Susie Cooper Ceramics [175]
18 Church Street
London NW8 8EP
T 7723 1555
F 7735 8309
E gallery1930@aol.com
W www.susiecooperceramics.com

Gary Anderson [63]
36 Chiltern Street
London W1U 7QJ
T/F 7224 2241
W www.garyanderson.com

Geffrye Museum [94]
Kingsland Road
London E2 3EA
T 7739 9893

F 7729 5647
E info@geffrye-museum.org.uk
W www.geffrye-museum.org.uk

Geo F. Trumper [44]
9 Curzon Street
London W1J 5HQ
T 7499 1850
E enquiries@trumpers.com
W www.trumpers.com

The George Inn [105]
77 Borough High Street
London SE1 1NH
T 7407 2056

Georgina von Etzdorf [37]
4 Ellis Street
London SW1X 9AL
T 7259 9715
W www.gve.co.uk

Get Stuffed [82]
105 Essex Road
London N1 2SL
T 7226 1364 / 07831 260 062
F 7359 8253
E taxidermy@thegetstuffed.co.uk
W www.thegetstuffed.co.uk
Afternoons only, ring ahead

Ghost [25]
36 Ledbury Road
London W11 2AB
T 7229 1057
F 7792 9794
W www.ghost.co.uk

Gill Wing Shops [81]
182, 190, 194 & 196 Upper Street
London N1 1RQ
T/F 7359 7697

Gina [37]
189 Sloane Street
London SW1X 9QR
T 7235 2932
F 7838 9720
W www.ginashoes.com

Ginger [23]
115 Westbourne Grove
London W2 4UP
T 7908 1990
F 7908 1991

Ginka [30]
137 Fulham Road
London SW3 6SD
T 7589 4866
F 7589 4877

Gordon's Wine Bar [151]
47 Villiers Street
London WC2N 6NE
T 7930 1408

Great Eastern Dining Rooms [159]
54–56 Great Eastern Street
London EC2A 3QR
T 7613 4545
F 7613 4137
W www.greateasterndining.co.uk

The Grill Room at the Dorchester [136]
53 Park Lane
London W1A 2HJ
T 7629 8888
F 7409 0114
E reservations@dorchesterhotel.com
W www.dorchesterhotel.com

The Guinea [47]
30 Bruton Place
London W1J 6NL
T   7499 1210

Hakkasan [133]
8 Hanway Place
London W1P 9DH
T   7907 1888
F   7907 1889
E   mail@hakkasan.com

Harvie & Hudson [167]
97 Jermyn Street
London SW1Y 6JE
T   7839 3578
F   7839 7020
E   info@harvieandhudson.com
W   www.harvieandhudson.com

The Havelock Tavern [25]
57 Masbro Road
London W14 0LS
T   7603 5374
E   info@thehavelocktavern.co.uk
W   www.thehavelocktavern.co.ui

Hazlitt's [114]
6 Frith Street
Soho Square
London W1D 3JA
T   7434 1771
F   7439 1524
E   reservations@hazlitts.co.uk
W   www.hazlittshotel.com

Her House [76]
30D Great Sutton Street
London EC1V 0DU
T   7689 0606
W   www.herhouse.uk.com
12–7 pm, Wednesday–Friday

Home [94]
100–106 Leonard Street
London EC2A 4RH
T   7684 8618
F   7684 1491
W   www.homebar.co.uk

Howarth Woodwind Specialists [63]
31–35 Chiltern Street
London W1U 7PN
T   7935 2407
F   7224 2564
E   sales@howarth.uk.com
W   www.howarth.uk.com

Hoxton Apprentice [94]
16 Hoxton Square
London N1 6NT
T   7749 2828
W   www.hoxtonapprentice.co.uk

Hoxton Square Bar and Kitchen [159]
2–4 Hoxton Square
London N1 6NU
T   7613 0709

Inn the Park [149]
St James's Park
London SW1A 2BJ
T   7451 9999
W   www.innthepark.com

Institute of Contemporary Arts (ICA) [57]
The Mall
London SW1Y 5AH
T   7930 6393
W   www.ica.org.uk

Isola [155]
145 Knightsbridge
London SW1X 7PA
T   7838 1044

J. Floris [167]
89 Jermyn Street
London SW1Y 6JH
T   0845 702 3239
E   fragrance@florislondon.com
W   www.florislondon.com

J. J. Fox & Robert Lewis [48]
19 St James's Street
London SW1A 1ES
T   7930 3787
F   7495 0097
W   www.jjfox.co.uk

J. Sheekey [50]
28–32 St Martin's Court
London WC2N 4AL
T   7240 2565

The Jacksons [20]
5 All Saints Road
London W11 1HA
T   7792 8336
F   7792 5687
E   enquiries@thejacksons.co.uk
W   www.thejacksons.co.uk

Jamaica Wine House [89]
12 St Michael's Alley
London EC3V 9DS
T   7626 9496

James Smith & Son Umbrellas [68]
55 New Oxford Street
London WC1A 1BL
T   7836 4731
W   www.james-smith.co.uk

Janet Reger [38]
2 Beauchamp Place
London SW3 1NG
T   7584 9368
F   7581 7946
E   info@janetreger.com
W   www.janetreger.co.uk

Jess James [51]
3 Newburgh Street
London W1F 7RE
T   7437 0199
F   7437 7001
E   jess@jessjames.com
W   www.jessjames.com

Jo Malone [35]
150 Sloane Street
London SW1X 9BX
T   7730 2100
E   info@jomalone.co.uk
W   www.jomalone.co.uk

Joe Tan [81]
98 Caledonian Road
London N1 9DN
T/F 7837 3885

John Lobb [162]
88 Jermyn Street
London SW1Y 6JD
T   7930 8089
F   7839 0981
E   shop@johnlobb.co.uk

Joie [69]
10 Museum Street
London WC1A 1JS
T/F 7497 5650

Julie's [18]
135 Portland Road
London W11 4LW
T   7727 7985
F   7229 4050
W   www.juliesrestaurant.com

Junky [90]
12 Dray Walk, Truman Brewery
91 Brick Lane
London E1 6RF
T   7247 1883
E   junky.styling@virgin.net
W   www.junkystyling.co.uk

The King's Head [81]
115 Upper Street
London N1 1QN
T   7226 1916
W   www.kingsheadtheatre.org

Knightsbridge Hotel [122]
10 Beaufort Gardens
London SW3 1PT
T   7584 6300
F   7584 6355
E   knightsbridge@firmdale.com
W   www.knightsbridgehotel.com

Koh Samui [57]
65 Monmouth Street
London WC2 9DT
T   7240 4280
F   7240 3232

Labour and Wait [90]
18 Cheshire Street
London E2 6EH
T   7729 6253
E   info@labourandwait.co.uk
W   www.labourandwait.co.uk
Friday by appointment
Saturday 1 pm–5 pm
Sunday 10 am–5 pm

Lara Bohinc 107 [170]
51 Hoxton Square
London N1 6NU
T   7684 1465
E   info@larabohinc107.co.uk
W   www.larabohinc107.co.uk

LASSCO St Michaels [93]
St Michael's Church, Mark Street
London EC2A 4ER
T   7749 9944
F   7749 9941
E   st.michaels@lassco.co.uk
W   www.lassco.co.uk

Le Taj [90]
134 Brick Lane
London E1 6RU
T   7247 4210
96 Brick Lane
London E1 6RL
T   7247 4210
W   www.letaj.co.uk

Leighton House Museum [25]
12 Holland Park Road
London W14 8LZ
T   7602 3316
W   www.rbkc.gov.uk/
    LHLeightonHouse

Le Pont de la Tour [105]
The Butlers Wharf Building
36d Shad Thames
London SE1 2YE
T   7403 8403
F   7940 1835
W   www.conran-restaurants.co.uk

Lesley Craze Gallery [75]
33–35a Clerkenwell Green
London EC1R 0DU
T   7608 0393
F   7251 5655
E   mail@lesleycrazegallery.co.uk
W   www.lesleycrazegallery.co.uk

Les Trois Garçons [94]
1 Club Row
London E1 6JX
T   7613 1924
F   7613 3067
E   info@lestroisgarcons.com
W   www.lestroisgarcons.com

Liberty [44]
214–20 Regent Street
London W1B 5AH
T   7734 1234
F   7573 9876
W   www.liberty.co.uk

Lindsay House [135]
21 Romilly Street
London W1D 5AF
T   7439 0450
W   www.lindsayhouse.co.uk

Liquid [159]
8 Pitfield Street
London N1 6HA
T   7729 0082

Liza Bruce [37]
9 Pont Street
London SW1X 9EJ
T   7235 8423

London Eye [100]
Jubilee Gardens
London SE1 7BP
T   0870 5000 600
W   www.londoneye.com

London Harpsichord Centre [63]
14 Chiltern Street
London W1U 7PY
T   7935 0789

London Silver Vaults [66]
53–64 Chancery Lane
London WC2A 1QS
T   7242 3844

The Lonsdale [155]
48 Lonsdale Road
London W11 2DE
T   7727 1517
W   www.thelonsdale.co.uk

Lulu Guinness [37]
3 Ellis Street
London SW1X 9AL
T   7823 4828
F   7823 4889
W   www.luluguinness.com

Maggie Jones [25]
6 Old Court Place
Kensington Church Street
London W8 4PL
T   7937 6462
F   7376 0510

Magma [57]
8 Earlham Street
London WC2H 9RY
T   7240 8498
E   enquiries@magmabooks.com
W   www.magmabooks.com

Maharishi [54]
19 Floral Street
London WC2E 9HL
T 7836 3860
F 7836 3857
E store@emaharishi.com
W www.emaharishi.com

The Main House [128]
6 Colville Road
London W11 2BP
T 7221 9691
W www.themainhouse.co.uk

The Mall [81]
359 Islington High Street
London N1 0PD

Manolo Blahnik [163]
49–51 Old Church Street
London SW3 5BS
T 7352 3863 or 7352 8622
F 7351 7314

Manor [20]
6–8 All Saints Road
London W11 1HH
T 7243 6363
E mail@manorw11.com

Map House [38]
54 Beauchamp Place
London SW3 1NY
T 7589 4325 or 7584 8559
F 7589 1041
E maps@themaphouse.com
W www.themaphouse.com

Marcus Campbell Art Books [102]
43 Holland Street
London SE1 9JR
T 7261 0111
E campbell@
marcuscampbell.demon.co.uk
W www.marcuscampbell.
demon.co.uk

Mary Moore [18]
5 Clarendon Cross
London W11 4AP
T 7229 5678

Marx Memorial Library [75]
37a Clerkenwell Green
London EC1R 0DU
T 7253 1485
F 7251 6039
E marxlibrary@britishlibrary.net
W www.marxmemoriallibrary.
sageweb.com

Matthew Williamson [47]
28 Bruton Street
London W1J 6QH
T 7629 6200
W www.matthewwilliamson.co.uk

Medcalf [77]
40 Exmouth Market
London EC1 4QE
T 7833 3533

Medicine Bar [159]
89 Great Eastern Street
London EC2A 3HX
T 7739 5173
E medicine@medicinebar.net
W www.medicinebar.net

Melbo Couture [63]
39 Chiltern Street
London W1U 7pp
T 7935 8055
W www.melboshoes.co.uk

Miller Harris [23]
14 Needham Road
London W11 2RP
T 7221 1545
F 7221 4370
E info@millerharris.com
W www.millerharris.com

Mint [63]
70 Wigmore Street
London W1U 2SF
T 7224 4406
F 7224 4407
E info@mint-shop.co.uk

Momo [133]
25 Heddon Street
London W1B 4BH
T 7434 4040
F 7287 0404
E momoresto@aol.com

Moro [77]
34–36 Exmouth Market
London EC1R 4QE
T 7833 8336
F 7833 9338
E info@moro.co.uk

Neal's Yard Dairy [57]
17 Shorts Gardens
London WC2H 9UP
T 7240 5700
E mailorder@nealsyarddairy.co.uk

Neal's Yard Remedies [57]
15 Neal's Yard
London WC2H 9DP
T 7379 7222
F 7379 0705
W www.nealsyardremedies.com

Newman Arms [66]
23 Rathbone Street
London W1P 1NH
T 7636 1127
F 7580 5878
E info@newmanarms.co.uk
W www.newmanarms.co.uk

Number 10 [17]
10 Golborne Road
London W10 5PE
T 8969 8922
W www.number10london.com

Oki Ni [169]
25 Savile Row
London W1S 3PR
T 7494 1716
W www.oki-ni.com

The Old Queen's Head [82]
44 Essex Road
London N1 8LN
T 7354 9273

Old Vic Theatre [105]
Waterloo Road
London SE1
T 870 060 6628
W www.oldvictheatre.com

Olivia Morris [17]
355 Portobello Road
London W10 5SA
T 8962 0353
E info@oliviamorrisshoes.com
W www.oliviamorrisshoes.com

Overdose on Design [90]
182 Brick Lane
London E1 6SP
T/F 7613 1266

E shop@overdoseondesign.com
W www.overdoseondesign.com

Oxo Tower [100]
Bargehouse Street
London SE1 9PH
T 7803 3888
W www.oxotower.co.uk

Ozer [63]
4–5 Langham Place
Regent Street
London W1A 3DG
T 7323 0505
F 7323 0111

Ozwald Boateng [166]
9 Vigo Street
London W1X 1AL
T 7437 0620
E shop@bespokecoutureltd.co.uk
W www.ozwaldboateng.co.uk

Palette London [82]
21 Canonbury Lane
London N1 2AS
T 7288 7428
W www.palette-london.com

Passione [64]
10 Charlotte Street
London W1T 2IT
T 7636 2833
W www.passione.co.uk

Paul Smith [164]
Westbourne House
122 Kensington Park Road
London W11 2EP
T 7727 3553
40–44 Floral Street [54]
London WC2E 9DS
T 7379 7133
W www.paulsmith.co.uk

Pauric Sweeney [92]
25a Pitfield Street
London N1 6HB
T/F 7253 5150

Philip Somerville [63]
38 Chiltern Street
London W1U 7QR
T 7224 1517
F 7486 5885

Philip Treacy [171]
69 Elizabeth Street
London SW1W 9PJ
T 7824 8787
F 7824 8262
W www.philiptreacy.co.uk

Pied à Terre [64]
34 Charlotte Street
London W1
T 7636 1178 / 07714 293 026
W www.pied-a-terre.co.uk

The Pineal Eye [52]
49 Broadwick Street
London W1F 9QR
T/F 7434 2567

The Pitfield Beer Shop [92]
14 Pitfield Street
London N1 6EY
T 7739 3701
W www.pitfieldbeershop.co.uk

Poetry Café [53]
22 Betterton Street
London WC2H 9BX
T 7420 9880

F 7240 4818
W www.poetrysociety.org.uk

The Portrait Restaurant [148]
The National Portrait Gallery
St Martin's Place
London WC2H 0HE
T 7312 2490
W www.npg.org.uk

Preen [17]
Unit 5, Portobello Green Arcade
281 Portobello Road
London W10 5TZ
T 8968 1542

Princes and Piccadilly Arcades [48]
off Jermyn Street
London W1

Quality Chop House [76]
92–94 Farringdon Road
London EC1R 3EA
T 7837 5093
F 7833 8748
E thequalitychophouse@
claranet.com

R. K. Stanley's [64]
6 Little Portland Street
London W1W 7JE
T 7462 0099
F 7462 0088

Rachel Riley [37]
14 Pont Street
London SW1X 9EN
T 7935 7007
F 7935 7004
E enquiries@rachelriley.co.uk
W www.rachelriley.com

Rasa Samudra [64]
5 Charlotte Street
London W1T 1RE
T 7637 0222
W www.rasarestaurants.com

Rasoi Vineet Bhatia [143]
10 Lincoln Street
London SW3 2TS
T 7225 1881
F 7581 0220
W www.vineetbhatia.com

Red Fort [142]
77 Dean Street
London W1D 3SH
T 7437 2525
F 7434 0721
E info@redfort.co.uk
W www.redfort.co.uk

Rellik [174]
8 Golborne Road
London W10 5NW
T/F 8962 0089

Richard James [165]
29 Savile Row
London W1S 2EY
T 7434 0605
F 7287 2265
E mail@richardjames.co.uk
W www.richardjames.co.uk

Roka [64]
37 Charlotte Street
London W1T 1RR
T 7580 6464

Rokit [53]
42 Shelton Street